UNDERSTANDING TEACHERS: A LIFE HISTORY APPROACH

Andrew C Sparkes

Designed & Desktop Published by
Michael Still (0392) 264850

RESEARCH SUPPORT UNIT
EDUCATIONAL RESEARCH MONOGRAPH SERIES

First published 1994 by The Research Support Unit
©Text Andrew C Sparkes, 1994

ISBN 85068 142 1

Cover design by Michael Still

Other books in the series:

1. **An Introduction to Research Methodology and Paradigms**
   Paul Ernest
3. **Analysing a Qualitative Interview**
   Hilary Radnor
4. **Writing up a Dissertation**
   Ken Shaw
5. **Case Study as Educational Research**
   Michael Golby

Further copies and others in the series available from:

School of Education, University of Exeter
Research Support Unit, Heavitree Road
Exeter EX1 2LU
Tel: (0392) 264781

INTRODUCTION TO THE MONOGRAPH SERIES

Education is concerned with the personal pursuit of knowledge and understanding. It is about the development of personal capacities and skills to enable individuals to realise their potential so that they can play an active role in creating satisfactory lives for themselves in an increasingly complex and pluralistic society. To meet the needs of individuals in our fast changing technological world educative policies and principles need to be under constant review and in this process educational research plays an important part.

The educational profession is constantly engaged in coping with change and many professionals seek to take a pro-active part in educational development, research and change. It is for such professionals who choose educational research as a means to this end that this series is designed.

They are called monographs because each one is the separate treatise of an individual active researcher in the School of Education, University of Exeter sharing his/her research experience and expertise with you. We do not seek to preach but to inform through our practice particular ways of researching in the field of education. We believe as a research community that there are many ways to achieve better quality education for all and each of us explore a particular path recognising with respect and humility the paths of others who pursue research with equal integrity and worth.

We share our philosophies, principles practices and processes of educational research with you and welcome you in joining us in the educational research endeavour.

Hilary A Radnor PhD
Series Editor

CONTENTS

PREFACE

> *How can we live without our lives? How will we know it's us without our past?*
> (Steinbeck, 1939, The Grapes of Wrath, p. 101)
>
> *There are few things more fascinating or informative than learning about the experience of other conscious beings as they make their way through the world. Accounts of their lives have a power to move us deeply, to help us imagine what it must be like in different social and historical circumstances, to provide insights into the workings of lives, and perhaps to provide a frame of reference for reassessing our own experience, own fortunes, own possibilities of existence.*
> (Runyan, 1982, p. 3)

The lives of others are inherently interesting and knowing about them can help us to see the world, and ourselves, in novel and different ways. Accordingly, this monograph explores ideas relating to the study of teachers' lives. Given the limitations of space that go with a monograph format I make no attempt to give wide coverage to the many complex theoretical and methodological issues associated with life history research. The more motivated reader can follow up some of these by selecting from the annotated bibliography that is provided. My intentions, for the moment, are more limited. What I hope to do is to provide some reference points for understanding the nature of life history research and what it has to offer us in making sense of teachers and teaching. I begin by giving a brief history of life history research in order to give this approach a sense of time and place. The contemporary importance of such research, as a way of articulating the voices of teachers and bringing them out of the shadows, is then signalled by looking at the images of the teacher that have prevailed in recent years. Following this, some of the strengths of the life history approach are considered and these are developed with regard to the need to contextualise the individual life story in a wider socio-historical framework. Having covered these key issues, I then attempt to illustrate life history research in action by drawing upon my own life history work with physical education teachers. By exploring the dimensions of marginality that different people within this occupational group experience, and locating these experiences in a wider context, I attempt to give a sense of the descriptive and explanatory power of life history research. In focusing upon the lives of these teachers a range of ethical issues are signalled and some of these are considered in greater detail. Should you read your way through to the end of this monograph my hope is that, rather than feel cheated by the brevity with which I have had to deal with some issues, you will have got a flavour of the work which will motivate you to explore life history research in the future.

INTRODUCTION: A BRIEF HISTORY OF LIFE HISTORY RESEARCH

> *The telling of a tale of a life is no new business, and certainly not one confined to the social sciences.* (Plummer, 1983, p. 8)

Despite having deep roots in a variety of disciplines, life history research has had a chequered career (see Langness & Frank, 1981; Plummer, 1983; Watson & Watson-Franke, 1985). As Runyan (1982) comments, 'The historical study for the background of life histories is a complex one, as life histories have been studied with waxing and waning enthusiasm by psychologists, sociologists, anthropologists, and a number of political scientists throughout the twentieth century' (p. 9). Runyan goes on to suggest that within the social sciences it is possible to identify three periods in the study of life history. From the 1920s through World War II substantial interest was shown in life histories and the 'life history method' via the study of personal documents such as diaries, letters, and autobiographies. Within the field of sociology the monumental 5 volume work of Thomas & Znaniecki (1918-1920) on *The Polish Peasant in Europe and America* assisted greatly in gaining recognition for the life history approach. This acceptance was furthered by the pioneering work of the Chicago School of sociologists led by Robert Park during the 1920s &1930s who, drawing upon symbolic interactionist theory, established the study of lives as a *bona fide* research method.

Unfortunately, this rise to fame was not to last and Runyan (1982) suggests that, from World War II through to the mid 1960s, there was a significant decline in interest in the study of individual lives. This fall from grace has been attributed to various factors, among them the growth of interest in experimental and quantitative methods of inquiry. For example, Becker (1966) notes how during this period there was a greater concern for abstract theory, social structural variables, and hypothesis testing forms of research in the quest for clear-cut, statistically significant, findings in scholarly publications, dissertations, and grant proposals. Clearly, then as now, the fate of the life history approach is inextricably bound to the historical emergence of sociology as a discipline and in particular its quest for academic respectability. As Goodson (1983) recognises, life history studies often appeared to be only 'telling tales' and this was seen as a low status exercise in 'scientific' or 'academic' terms 'Set against the life history of the aspirant academic we clearly see the unattractiveness of the life history method' (P. 137). He also argues:

> *The pervasive drift of academic disciplines towards abstract theory has been irresistibly followed: in this evolutionary imperative, it is not difficult to discern the desire of sociologists to gain parity of esteem with other academic disciplines......Alongside the move towards abstract academic theory, sociological method became more 'professional'. Essentially this led towards a model of single study research..... But this dominant experimental model, so fruitful in analogies with other sciences, and hence so crucial in legitimating sociology as an academic discipline, led to the neglect of sociology's full range of methodology and data sources........life history and biography have remained at the sidelines of the sociological enterprise. (Goodson, 1988, pp. 76-77.)*

From approximately the mid-1960s to the present, Runyan (1982) believes that there has been, 'an enormous amount of work in the social sciences relating to the study of lives....There is, in short, an enormously rich and diverse tradition to draw upon.....with much work in recent years examining how the life course is influenced by social structural, demographic and historical conditions' (pp. 11-12). However, Plummer (1990) takes a more conservative view and talks of the minor resurgence of interest in life histories, across academic disciplines and national boundaries, that has taken place in the last decade. As is often the case in the world of educational research the renaissance of life histories has been somewhat delayed, and in 1985 Woods suggested that within this domain, 'Life histories are due for revival' (p. 13). Following the publication in 1985 of *Teachers' Lives and Careers* by Ball & Goodson, and *Teacher Careers* by Sikes, Measor & Woods, this minor revival now seems to be under way and increased attention is now being given to this form of research as a way of understanding teachers' lives, careers, cultures and life worlds, (For other examples see Butt, 1989; Butt &

Raymond, 1987; Goodson, 1981, 1983, 1991a & b, 1992a; Goodson & Walker, 1991; Schempp et al, 1993; Sparkes & Templin, 1992; Sparkes et al, 1990; Sparkes 1994 a & b; Woods, 1984, 1987). Of course, this is not to suggest that life history research has become fully accepted within the educational community. As Goodson (1992b) argues:

> *Studying teachers' lives will, I suspect, never become mainstream, for such study seeks to understand and to give voice to an occupational group that have been historically marginalised. Yet, as a group, teachers retain considerable power, and as is often the case much truth resides in the margins. This mode of study will undoubtedly contribute to the understanding of the educational endeavour but the use of such study has to be patrolled with extraordinary care. (p. 15).*

Bearing this in mind, there is a need to be aware of some of the reasons that the life history approach has been given the attention it has in recent years. First and foremost, this interest has developed alongside the growth of interpretive (qualitative) research in education, which acknowledges the subjective, multiple and partial nature of human experience (see Smith, 1989). Such a focus plays to a major strength of the life history approach that involves its ability to reveal the subjective realm of peoples' lives in ways that respect their uniqueness and allows them to speak for themselves. In many ways, life history research can begin to provide an antidote to the dominant images of teachers in the literature.

IMAGES OF TEACHERS IN THE LITERATURE -
SEEKING AN ANTIDOTE

Teachers, like all of us, have a past, a present, and aspirations for the future. Such a stance is far from original. As Benyon (1985) argues 'Unless we first understand teachers we can hardly claim to understand teaching' (p. 158). He warns that teachers in the past have too often been treated as though they were cardboard cut-outs which denies that behind the act of teaching there are embedded a range of attitudes, motives and emotions. Likewise, Connell (1985) notes how many sociological studies have 'tended to ignore the personal dimensions of teaching and often give an oddly inhuman account of this most human of jobs' (p. 4).

Both Ball & Goodson (1985) and Goodson (1992b) have provided overviews of the historical images that have been constructed of teachers. These scholars suggest that British research on teachers has moved through a number of contemporary phases.

> *In the 1960s teachers were shadowy figures on the educational landscape, mainly known, or unknown, through large scale surveys, or historical analyses of their position in society, the key concept of apprehending the practice of teaching was that of role.....Teachers were represented in aggregate through imprecise statistics or were viewed as individuals only as formal role incumbents mechanistically and unproblematically responding to the powerful expectations of their role set. (Ball & Goodson, 1985, pp. 6-7).*

During this period, researchers were concerned to explain differences in school performances which often led, under the persuasive sway of forms of cultural deprivation and social pathology theories, to the pupils being blamed for their own failures. In contrast, at the end of the 1960s case study researchers began to crack open the 'black box' of the school to look at schooling as a social process and the manner in which pupils were 'processed'. As Goodson (1992b) argues, this shift in research focus, from the point of view of the teacher, was not necessarily for the better. The concepts of labelling and typification dominated as frames for understanding the mechanisms of how teachers categorised and differentiated their pupils in ways that structured their career opportunities at school and life chances once they left. Consequently, this research emphasis shifted from 'blaming the pupil' to 'blaming the teacher'.

Teachers were implicated centrally not only in constructing differences in pupil performance but also in the maintenance and reproduction of gender stereotypes. Hence the sympathies of the researcher lay primarily with the pupils, working class and female pupils in particular, who were the 'under dogs' in the classroom, teachers were the villains of the piece. (Ball & Goodson, 1985, p. 7).

In the late 1970s another change occurred and attention shifted to the constraints within which teachers worked. In this scenario teachers were transformed from villains to 'victims' or 'dupes' of the system within which they had to operate. Neo-Marxists of the period emphasised the societal and economic determinants of education and were prone to portray teachers as 'puppets' of the capitalist state who were helpless agents in the reproduction of the relations of production. In contrast, the views of interactionist theorists emphasised the more immediate problems that teachers faced in resolving the dual demands of instruction and control in the classroom.

As the limitations inherent in both Marxist and interactionist approaches were recognized a more productive and dialectical conception of teachers' work has begun to emerge. The teacher is seen as involved in the development of creative, strategical responses to societal and situational constraints, or as resolving ever present dilemmas through and with their interaction with pupils. (Ball & Goodson, 1985, pp7-8).

Such moves began the process of recognising the complexity of the teachers' task and saw them more as human beings, rounded social actors, with their own problems, perspectives and aspirations. However, as Goodson (1981) pointed out, while the question of how teachers saw their work and lives was opened up in the late 1970s, he believed that researchers had still not confronted the complexity of the teacher as an active agent making his or her own history. Although many researchers had stopped treating teachers as numerical aggregates, historical footnotes, or problematic role incumbents, there was still a tendency to see them as interchangeable types unchanged by circumstance or time. This was particularly true of contemporary interactionism and ethnomethodological studies of schooling which Goodson (1983) saw as focusing on situation and occasion while giving little attention to the individual biography, personal views and life-styles of teachers. Consequently, teachers were presented as 'particular kinds of species reproducing within busy, tiring and unchanging environments.....in these accounts the teacher becomes depersonalised, neutral and above all eminently *interchangeable*: the same old teacher we know so well' (p. 140). The assumption of interchangeability was closely associated with the anti-historical assumption of timelessness, 'whatever the time, whoever the teacher, everything is much the same' (p. 140). In view of this, Goodson (1981) called for a more contextually sensitive research form that was founded on life history methods.

> *The pursuit of personal and biographical data might rapidly challenge the assumptions of interchangeability. Likewise, by tracing the teacher's life as evolved over time - throughout the teacher's career and through several generations - the assumption of timelessness might also be remedied.* **In understanding something so intensely personal as teaching it is critical we know about the person the teacher is.** *Our paucity of knowledge in this area is a manifest indictment of the range of our sociological imagination. (p. 69)*

More recently, Goodson (1991a) has drawn upon lessons learnt from folk music to suggest that those who sing the songs are more important than the songs themselves which cannot be understood without knowing something about the life of the singer. He comments 'to understand teacher development and curriculum development and to tailor it accordingly, we need to know a great deal more about teachers' priorities. We need in short to know more about teachers' lives' (p. 138). Yet, as we move towards the 21st century it would appear that we still know little about teachers' lives, even though it is they who play such a central role in the complex conundrum of schooling. Even more worrying are the suggestions by Goodson (1992b) that, given the changes in the patterns of political and administrative control over teachers in the 1980s, there is a real danger (in terms of power and invisibility) of teachers 'returning to the shadows' in the coming years. If this is the case then there is clearly a need for forms of research that locates the lives of teachers within a wider contextual understanding.

> *In an era of new reforms and attempts to restructure schools this literature becomes even more important. Studies of teachers' lives thereby re-assert the importance of the teacher: of knowing the teacher, of listening to the teacher and of speaking with the teacher......In such times, educational studies which re-assert the importance of the teacher's voice are particularly valuable in building a knowledgeable counter-culture to stand against some of the crude simplicities of political and 'managerial' views of schooling. (Goodson, 1992c, pp. 234-235).*

Given the images of the teacher that have been socially constructed within the research community, and given the dangers of a 'return to the shadows', then life history research has a part to play in acting as an antidote to the prevailing malaise. It can do this by articulating the teacher's voice and ensuring that this voice is heard loudly within the world of teacher development. Butt & Raymond (1987) acknowledge the potential of life histories to act as a vehicle for recording and interpreting the teacher's voice. They note:

> *It provides a vehicle for recording and interpreting the teacher's voice. The notion of the teacher's voice is used in several literal and metaphorical senses.......In a political sense, the teacher's voice attests to the right of speaking and being represented. It can represent the views of both unique individuals and a number of people - a collective voice. "Voice" also connotes that what is said is characteristic of teachers, as distinct from other potential voices. (p. 77).*

In relation to this Elbaz (1990) suggests that a concern with voice is implicit in the work of all those committed to the empowerment of teachers and that where the notion of 'voice' is used, 'the term is always used against the background of previous silence, and it is a political usage as well as an epistemological one' (p. 17). This is particularly so for teachers who, as an occupation, have been historically marginalised. Similarly, this is so for those groups within the teaching profession who have been marginalised such as physical education teachers, careers teachers, and women. With regard to the latter, feminist scholars have mounted a substantial challenge to this background of silence by recovering women's voices as part of a process that Marcus (1984) calls 'invisible mending'. As Munro (1991) comments:

> *In seeking a methodology which would allow for and value personal voice, be collaborative, and foster transformation, life history seems to present the most viable alternative......In addition to life history's usefulness for studying persons whose history has been marginalised, life histories are particularly well suited to illustrating some aspects of culture not usually portrayed by other means, such as women's view of their culture. (pp. 3-4).*

The ability of life history research to articulate the voices of teachers is a major strength of this approach to understanding. There are other strengths that need to be noted.

13

SOME STRENGTHS AND WEAKNESSES OF LIFE HISTORY RESEARCH

> *Life history research advocates, first and foremost, a concern with the phenomenal role of lived experience, with the ways in which members interpret their own lives and the world around them......There are many ways of getting at the phenomenology of experience, but in the end there is probably no substitute for spending many hours talking with the subject, gathering up his or her perceptions of the world, encouraging these to be written down, reading through letters and diaries, and developing an intensive intimate familiarity with one concrete life. (Plummer, 1983, p. 67).*

The quotation given above by Plummer indicates that life history research needs to be seen as a broad approach to understanding that incorporates a range of data gathering techniques to make sense of lives. In his excellent book *Documents of Life*, Plummer (1983) includes the following possible documents that can be used to generate insights into the lives of others: diaries, letters, 'Vox Populi' and guerrilla journalism, oral histories, 'the literature of fact', photographs, and films/videos. He concludes, 'For here are a whole battery of research tools, widely ignored and neglected in both research texts and courses, which have enormous potential for exploring concrete social experience in humanistic fashion. They can be put together in various combinations' (p. 35).

Clearly, there is no one single life history method or technique but rather a range of strategies. This point is emphasised by Faraday and Plummer (1979) who in their own study drew upon data from a range of sources that included: letters (solicited and unsolicited), interviews (focused and unfocused), observations (covert and overt), books (autobiographical, pornographic, novels and books authored by their subjects), and diaries. These strategies can be used to focus upon an individual or upon groups. In the latter an attempt is made to explore the commonalities that often emerge across many life histories. Therefore, just using a set of prescribed techniques does not make for good life history research. As Wolcott (1990) reminds us in connection with ethnography:

*The most noteworthy thing about ethnographic research techniques is their lack of noteworthiness.....There is no way one could ever hope to produce an ethnography simply by employing many, or even all, of the techniques that ethnographers use. Ethnography......is **not** a reporting process guided by a specific set of techniques. It is an inquiry process carried out by human beings.......it is not the techniques employed that make a study ethnographic, but neither is it necessarily what one looks at; the critical element is interpreting what one has seen. (pp. 191-202).*

The issue of interpretation as central to life history research clearly signals its allegiance to the *interpretive* (qualitative) research paradigm (see Smith, 1989; Sparkes, 1992a). As Marsick (1989) comments 'Life history as a qualitative research methodology highlights the concerns of the interpretive tradition in which it is rooted for reporting the perspectives of people in the situation being studied' (p. 1). Illuminating the insider perspective is of great importance in any attempt to explain why people act in certain ways rather than others. According to Burrell & Morgan (1979), 'The interpretive paradigm is informed by a concern to understand the world as it is, to understand the fundamental nature of the world at the level of subjective experience. It seeks explanation within the realm of consciousness and subjectivity, within the frame of reference of the participant as opposed to the observer of action' (p. 28). Within this paradigm Plummer (1983) suggests that interactionist theory and the personal document method have a strong affinity as both have an 'unrelenting focus on the importance of the subjective viewpoint' (p. 53). However, this is not to suggest that the life history approach is exclusive to any one theoretical domain and it has been used in recent years by a wide variety of researchers for different purposes. For example, the studies presented in Bertaux's (1981) *Biography and Society* draw upon diverse theoretical frameworks ranging from symbolic interactionism to structuralist Marxism. Consequently, the term 'life history' can take on different meanings depending upon the discipline of the individual and their particular perspective within that discipline (also see Goodson, 1992a).

Given the strong affinity between interactionism and life history work, it would seem appropriate at this stage to suggest some *strengths* of the life history approach for understanding teachers. To illustrate these strengths I combine the viewpoints of Plummer (1983) and Sikes et al (1985) in relation to how the notion of a career in teaching might be framed.

1 It focuses upon, takes seriously, and attempts to enter into the *subjective reality* of the teacher with a view to providing an intimately involved account of a life or lives. The structure and content of a career depends upon how the person concerned sees it. Consequently, the person's interests must be considered.

2 Rather than impose order and rationality upon the social world, life histories present a more ambiguous, complex and chaotic view of reality. While much of social science glosses over the central moments in our lives that revolve around indecision, turning points, confusions, contradictions and ironies, the life history takes these seriously in order to understand how they are played out in everyday life. As a consequence, life histories more than many other approaches are able to give meaning to the overworked notion of *process*.

In terms of a career in teaching this is concerned with on-going development that may involve immediate, short, or long-term perspectives. These may be clearly or hazily perceived and development may be multi-faceted with differential progress along different routes and differential realisation of interests.

3 While much social science is involved in the process of 'amputation', interpretive research in general, and life history research in particular, attempts to focus upon the *totality* of the biographical experience. This perspective constantly addresses and interlinks biological bodily needs, immediate social groups, personal definitions of the situation, and historical change in the life of an individual and in the outside world. As a consequence, the life history approach allows one to grasp some sense of the *totality* of a life.

In terms of a career in teaching this means that a *whole life view* needs to be adopted whereby careers are seen within the entire *longitudinal perspective of a life*. This is important since a person's interests, certain aspects of the self that formulate these interests, and the way that one attributes meanings to events - all these are *developed over time*. Therefore, we need to see sections of a career properly located within the dimension of a life-span. Likewise, a whole personal world view needs to be adopted which considers all of a person's interests and activities both in and out of school. This is the *latitudinal dimension* to a career. The segments of a career need to be located within this whole if we are to understand the nature and importance within a person's life. Both the longitudinal and the latitudinal perspectives further assist in gaining a sense of *process*.

4 As individuals live their lives they move persistently through history and structure. As a consequence, life history research constantly has to move between the changing biographical history of the individual and the social history of his or her life span. Therefore, a life history cannot be told without constant reference to historical change. This central focus on *change* is a major strength of life history research as is its ability to bestride the *micro-macro* interface. In studying a life history one has to consider its historical context and the dialectical relationship between self and society as individuals come to terms with the imperatives of social structures. Therefore, from a collection of life histories that are grounded in personal biography, there is the possibility of discerning what is general across cases in order for links to be made with more macro theories.

Such issues are easier to grasp if we consider the stories told by a newly qualified teacher and a teacher who has just retired after a full career in teaching. To make sense of their experiences, both similar and dissimilar, we would need to locate them in a historical context. For example, the retired teacher's experiences might have been shaped by the 1944 Education Act while the newly qualified teacher is sure to be shaped by the 1988 Educational Reform Act. Each of these Acts came about for specific reasons that are located within the wider social, economic and political structures beyond, yet intimately entwined with, the lives of each individual teacher in ways that shape their careers and how they operate in schools.

5 Life histories provide insights into a person's *identity* and sense of *self*, and the manner in which these develop and change over time.

To the above strengths we need to add the potential of life history research to facilitate a *collaborative* mode of engagement in which much of the *control* within the research process is given to the teacher. In relation to this Goodson (1991b) has expressed concern over those who wish to develop collaborative modes of research that give full equality and stature to the teacher but who then focus upon the practice of teachers as the initial and predominant focus. He argues that for the researcher this focus may seem quite unproblematic; however, for the teacher it may seem to be the maximum point of vulnerability. For him a more valuable, and less vulnerable, entry point would be to examine teachers' work in the context of their lives since this focus potentially allows the teacher greater authority and control over the research process.

> *Talking about her or his own life the teacher is, in this specific sense, in a less immediately exposed situation; and the 'exposure' can be more carefully, consciously and personally controlled. (This is not, it should be noted, to argue that once again 'exploitation' might not take place, nor that there are no longer major ethical questions to do with exposure.) But I think this starting point has substantive as well as strategic advantages. (Goodson, 1991b, p. 148).*

By creating knowledge that carries the teacher's voice the life history approach also has the potential to overcome several of the problems that have been associated with much of the previous research on teachers. In summarising these problems Woods (1987) suggests, amongst other things, that much of this research has not produced knowledge *for* teachers but for others in a way that is remote from the practical concerns of teachers. Furthermore, such knowledge is not under their control 'It is produced "out there" and "up there" on an apparently superior plane in forms and terms which they cannot engage....Teachers are small cogs in the mighty wheel. Their own views on the matter do not appear to count' (pp. 121-122). Likewise, the input of a teacher's own personal resources and the degree to which teachers can change situations as well as themselves are largely left out of the account. In view of all this, it is hardly surprising that many teachers define much educational research as irrelevant. In contrast, while not a panacea for all the problems associated with educational research, the life history approach offers teachers access to research, control over it, and it can provide results that have personal meanings in their lives.

Therefore, as Woods (1987) argues life histories have a definite part to play in the 'construction of a meaningful, relevant and living teacher knowledge' (p. 132). Importantly, in relation to this construction, Goodson (1992c) believes that because in the development of life histories, teachers are involved in work that is able to illuminate and feed back into the practice, conditions and understandings of their working lives, we might be able to develop a paradigm where researcher and teacher understanding move forward in harmony. That is, an extended paradigm of educational enquiry where teachers could become both a central focus for, and active agents in, the undertaking of educational enquiry.

ON THE NEED TO CONTEXTUALISE LIVES

Of course, with regard to orthodox forms of quantitative research underpinned by positivistic and post-positivistic assumptions there are a range of 'weaknesses' inherent in life history research. Here, the issue of generalizability or representativeness is a useful example. After all, what can be gained from the intense study of one person's life? What can it tell us about the lives of others? Some would say very little! However, there are several responses available. The first is to reject wholeheartedly the epistemological and ontological assumptions that underpin more orthodox research forms, and to point out that interpretive research draws on a radically different set of assumptions. As a consequence different criteria are required to judge the products of interpretive inquiry (see Smith, 1989, 1993; Sparkes 1992a). This is an important issue for another reason. As Plummer (1983) points out, life history research is often the strategy of the poor, of those researchers who have little hope, and I would add desire, of gaining a large and representative sample from which to make bold, grand generalizations. As such, the standard concerns of traditional sampling procedures are not really an issue in life history work. The real questions revolve around who, from all the people available, are to be selected for such a labour intensive study? Here, Sears (1992) provides a telling comment.

> Our culture's fondness for generalizations.....our fetish for numbers, ranging from IQ to sports statistics, may lead some people to question the value of interviewing only a few people. The power of qualitative data, however, lies not in the number of people interviewed but in the researcher's ability to know well a few people in their cultural contexts. The test of qualitative inquiry is not the unearthing of a seemingly endless multitude of unique individuals but illuminating the lives of a few well-chosen individuals. The ideographic often provides greater insight than the nomothetic. (p.148).

Of course this is not to deny the complex and important issues associated with using one life to gain insights into the lives of others. Such issues certainly need to be addressed. As Plummer (1983) notes:

> *One of the most apparent attacks on life history research is that it fails to provide representative cases and thus hurls the reader into the eccentric world of the atypical - a story in itself, but no more. To avoid this accusation, the researcher must work out and explicitly state the life history's relationship to a wider population, and thus the issue of ideographic and nomothetic social science re-raises its head. (p. 100).*

Similarly, Faraday & Plummer (1979) note that while life histories may provide the 'truth' about immediate experience, they need not necessarily provide 'the truth' about the location of that immediate experience in the wider structure. Therefore, the need to *contexualize* the individual life history is crucial. A useful way to illustrate this point is to explore the differences between the life *story* and the life *history*. Often, these two terms are condensed as in the following definition.

> *As we see it, the "life history" is any retrospective account by an individual of his life in whole or part, in written or oral form, **that has been elicited or prompted by another person**...... We use the term "autobiography", by contrast, to refer to a person's **self-initiated** account of his life, which is usually but not always in written form. (Watson & Watson-Franke, p. 2).*

In contrast, Corradi (1991) argues that life stories focus exclusively upon *oral* accounts.

> *In sociology, the term 'life stories' refers to the results of a research approach that consists of collecting an individual's oral account of his or her life or of special aspects of it; the narrative is initiated by a specific request from the researcher and the ensuing dialogue is directed by the latter towards his or her field of inquiry. A life story thus involves a dialogical interactive situation in which the course of an individual's life is given shape: by reason of the request that stirs and orientates them, and the subsequent analysis to which the researcher subjects them, life stories aim to explain and give meaning to social phenomena. (p. 106).*

Goodson (1992c) further emphasises the basic distinctions between a life story and a life history. The former is seen as the 'story we tell about our life', while the latter is a collaborative venture reviewing a wider range of evidence. Consequently, the life history is the life story located in its historical context.

The life story is a personal reconstruction of experience in this case by the teacher. 'Life story givers' provide data for the researcher often in loosely structured interviews. The researcher seeks to elicit the teacher's perceptions and stories but is generally passive rather than actively interrogative......The life history also begins with the life story that the teacher tells but seeks to build on the information provided. Hence other people's accounts might be elicited, documentary evidence and a range of historical data amassed. The concern is to develop a wide intertextual and intercontextual mode of analysis. This provision of a wider range of data allows a contextual background to be constructed. (p. 243).

Clearly, the contextualisation that Goodson (1992c) calls for is necessary if links are to be made to the lives of other people. Furthermore, such contextualisation guards against the tendency to focus so intently on the individual that a kind of blindness results that divorces personal experience from the wider socioeconomic and political structures that shape them. This means, for example, that in studying teachers' careers there is a need to consider both the subjective and objective dimensions. As Ball & Goodson (1985) remind us:

By definition individual careers are socially constructed and individually experienced over time. They are subjective trajectories through historical periods and at the same time contain their own organising principles and distinct phases. However, there are important ways in which individual careers can be tied to wider political and economic events. In some cases particular historical 'moments' or periods assume special significance in the construction of or experience of a career. (p. 11).

In a similar vein Acker (1989) comments:

Individuals called teachers face a structure of opportunities outside of their control. Their chances of achieving the rewards offered by these structures, should they want them, are significantly altered at different times in history. Demographic changes resulting in falling or rising school rolls; social changes in the acceptability of married women and mothers working outside the home; the age structure of teachers or academics now in post (a consequence of earlier social events); political decisions about expansion or contraction of certain curriculum subjects or extensions of education to younger or older children or adults - all these produce what feel like historical accidents to individuals who are relatively advantaged or disadvantaged by their operation. (p. 9).

What this means is that any individual teacher's career is constructed, constrained, and shaped within a shifting and interconnected matrix of historical, demographic, economic and political structures. Very often we are only dimly aware of how these social structures operate upon us, but they operate nonetheless and at times their impact upon the lives of teachers is dramatic and powerful. Therefore, it is limiting to simply view teachers as calculating individuals who make their decisions in a sociopolitical vacuum. Equally, it is inappropriate to view teachers simply as cogs in a machine who are unable to influence the circumstances that shape their work (see Sparkes, 1991). As Giddens' (1979) notion of *structuration* suggests, social structures are both constituted by human agency, and at the same time are the very medium of that constitution. He argues:

> *Power relations therefore are always two-way, even if the power of one actor or party in a social relation is minimal compared to another. Power relations are relations of autonomy and dependence, but even the most autonomous agent is in some degree dependent, and the most dependent actor or party in a relationship retains some autonomy. (Giddens, 1979, p. 93).*

In order to gain a sense of the dialectical process that exists between the agency of individuals and the constraints of social structures, there is a need to integrate situational forms of analysis with those that focus upon biographical and historical strands. Such an integration, according to Goodson (1981), would move studies away from a position where 'the human actor is located and studied in a manner contrively divorced from the previous history of both the actor and the situation' (p. 69). In this sense the contextualisation of life stories via life histories can actually assist in illuminating and throwing into sharp relief the wider social formations. As Faraday & Plummer (1979) comment:

> *When one conducts a life history interview the findings become alive in terms of historical processes and structural constraints. People do not wander round the world in a timeless, structureless limbo. They themselves acknowledge the importance of historical factors and structural constraints.....The analysis of life histories actually pushes one first of all to the problem of constraints bearing down upon the construction of any life. (p. 780).*

Therefore, life history research can assist in making connections between personal troubles and social issues. As Woods (1987) notes, 'Life histories can inform our thinking about the personal engagement with social structure, with implications for some of the most prominent public issues of the day' (p. 130). This potential of life histories needs to be developed in order to guard against the production of accounts that focus exclusively upon personal process and experiences at the expense of any consideration of socio-historical structures. In relation to this, Goodson (1988) warns, 'The life historian must constantly broaden the concern with personal truth to take account of the wider socio-historical concerns *even if these are not part of the consciousness of the individual*' (p. 80). This broadened concern forces a consideration of the contextual parameters that substantially impinge upon and constantly restrict the teacher's life. Such a concern, for Goodson (1992b) leads to the development of both a *narrative of action* and a history or *genealogy of context*, that in combination allows life history research to overcome the accusations of non-generalizability by moving beyond the individual life story in a theoretically powerful and vibrant manner.

LIFE HISTORY RESEARCH IN ACTION - GLIMPSES OF MARGINAL WORLDS

So how might some of what has been said about life history research work out in practice? What does life history research produce? To give a flavour of this kind of work I will draw upon some of my own life history research with physical education (PE) teachers in England. The motivations for this study are rooted in my own life history that includes time as a PE teacher in secondary schools where I never came to terms with the marginal status ascribed to both PE as a subject and the people who teach it. As a consequence, I became interested in how others involved in PE from different generations made sense of their existence in schools and so I began to collect their life stories. As I listened to these stories my own thoughts, images, and experiences of marginality became fragmented as I reflected on the tales I was told by others who were differently positioned. In a very real sense as I explored the life histories of others I was embarking on a simultaneous journey into my own life history, my own past, present, and future. This is not surprising, for as Sears (1992) points out, 'As we peer into the eyes of the other, we embark on a journey of the Self: exploring our fears, celebrating our voices, challenging our assumptions, reconstructing our pasts. Ultimately, qualitative inquiry is our method to search for personal meaning and understanding, (p. 155). The journey has been very unsettling so far.

Given that my life history work is still on-going (can it now ever end?) I will not attempt to provide comprehensive coverage of the many issues that have been raised so far (for more details see Schempp et al, 1993; Sparkes, 1990a, 1990b, 1992b, 1994 a & b; Sparkes & Bloomer, 1993; Sparkes & Templin, 1992; Sparkes & Tiihonen, 1992; Sparkes et al, 1990; Templin et al, 1991). My intentions in this monograph are more modest in that I will attempt to provide glimpses of marginal worlds in teaching by using moments from the life stories of PE teachers. These moments are then briefly contextualised to illustrate how life history research can locate individual lives within wider social structures that shape their lives in powerful ways, even though they are often beyond the consciousness of the individual.

First, however, there is a need to make some brief comments about how I gained access to these moments of lives. This, in turn, relates to issues of sampling. There is no particular reason for life history work not to be framed within the sampling strategies associated with more positivistic or orthodox research designs that deal in large numbers and random sampling. However, as Plummer (1983) comments:

> *Life history research is usually the strategy of the poor - of the researcher who has little hope of gaining a large and representative sample from which bold generalization may be made. The issue of traditional sampling strategies is hence not usually at stake; rather the problem becomes this: who from the teeming millions of world population is to be selected for such intensive study and sociological immortality? The great person, the common person, the marginal person? The volunteer, the selected, the coerced? (p. 87).*

Plummer (1983) then goes on to discuss several frames for selection which include formal criteria, and pragmatism and chance. With regard to the former in my own life history work several formal criteria were invoked. For example, only those who were, or had been, PE specialists would be interviewed. Similarly, since I wished to explore and understand how issues relating to marginality were perceived across generations this meant devising categories relating to age and career structure within teaching [1]. This in itself was more difficult than it seemed because it was difficult to define with precision what is meant by a 'career' in PE given that, for example, many emigrate from this subject as they approach middle age in order to teach more of their second subject and/or take up pastoral roles within the school. Therefore, while these teachers no longer teach PE, they are still linked to the trajectory of a career in PE which develops within specific structural constraints that often encourage and support such moves out of the subject. In view of this, I initially decided to interview male and female PE teachers from the following categories.

a   Student teachers
b   Inductees-probationers (in first year of teaching)
c   Early career (2-7 years)
d   Mid-career (8-19 years)
e   Late-career (20+ years and still teaching PE)
f   Retirement
    (i)   Retired from PE but employed in schools
    (ii) Retired from career in teaching/school employment
    (iii) Career change (held a teaching position, then decided to leave teaching for another profession)

26

Of course, this still meant I had to make choices about who I interviewed within each of these categories. Often such choices were related to the pragmatism and chance that Plummer (1983) highlights. For example, when I first began my life history work I was employed at a university in the Midlands. Part of my work there involved supervising PGCE PE students on their teaching practice in schools. Consequently, I visited a range of schools in the area and during these visits I invariably ended up in conversations with the PE staff where I got to know their views on life in general and PE in particular. I also got to hear about other schools and PE teachers in the area via this unofficial grapevine. These associations formed the basis for my initial selection of teachers to interview. The same process occurred when I moved from the Midlands to take up my current position at Exeter University. Once again, my visits to schools enabled me to lock into the local PE network which allowed me identify people within particular categories.

Having identified PE teachers who fell into different categories my choice of who to interview was based mainly on how well I interacted with specific people in schools, and how accessible they were in terms of time and place. Quite simply, as my research was not being funded, the distance the teacher lived from my home was a financially significant issue in terms of my petrol costs! Most often I would mention my life history work during a school visit to see if the teacher was interested in participating. At other times I would telephone PE teachers who I knew in order to outline my study and to see if they would be interested in participating. If there was a positive response I would then arrange an initial interview. Based on relevant information gained from my local network I would also contact some teachers 'cold', without first knowing them. For example, as my study developed I became aware that physical degeneration and physical injury were issues of major importance to some teachers and felt it would be interesting to interview some PE teachers who had left the profession completely, or had moved out of the subject into another role in the school, due to physical injury. One cold Autumn morning as I was watching a netball lesson, I became involved in a conversation with the teacher who was supervising the lesson and she mentioned that a former PE teacher in the school had left teaching due to an injury. After the lesson, over a coffee, I explained my life study project to this teacher and asked her if she would mind giving me the name and telephone number of the teacher she had mentioned.

This she did, and having contacted her ex-colleague by telephone, I am currently in the process of interviewing this individual whose teaching career was brought to an abrupt end by a physical injury. Such contacts clearly come about by chance but are none the less illuminating for that. As Plummer (1983) points out:

> *Many life history studies do not appear to be planned; a chance encounter, a subject of interest emerging from a wider study, an interesting volunteer - these seem common ways of finding a subject.........Given that much life history research will simply evolve piecemeal - often out of a wider study - it is unlikely that the researcher will usually be able to sit down quietly for two or three hours to work out precisely all the questions that need going over with the life history subject. Living with ambiguity is a central feature of life history research and there is no easy way to plan it. Thus for instance very frequently the life history subject will not appear as such until after a few months of acquaintance, and the question concerning the subject's participation in a life history study may take a long time before it can be broached. In an ideal world of course, the subject will be located and a contract worked out between researcher and subject which specifies the solutions to all kinds of problems; in practice the entire process is much more muddled and confused than that. (pp. 87-90).*

Despite its often muddling nature, there are frames that guide the process. For example, when inviting a teacher to become engaged in my project I always make the following points clear to them from the start.

(1)   My motivations for doing the study based on my experiences as a PE teacher and as someone who now works closely with PE students.

(2)   The time involved in life history work. Here, I emphasise that I will need at least three interviews of approximately one and a half hours each.

(3)   The interviews will be tape recorded.

(4)   The interviews are confidential and anything I write about the individual will use pseudonyms to protect their identity.

(5)   That they are the experts on their own life. There are no 'right' and 'wrong' answers. I am there as a learner, and I am not there to evaluate them in any way.

(6)   They had the right to read the transcripts of their interviews to check for accuracy (very few have ever chosen to do this).

When I do arrange interviews I always try and get to meet the teacher out of school. Given the hectic nature of the school day there is rarely much chance for PE teachers (or any other subject teacher) to find uninterrupted time to sit down and reflect upon their lives. At times there are no alternatives, and the subject will only be interviewed in school. For example, an ex-PE teacher who had moved out of the subject into a pastoral role and then on to deputy head teacher, had to be interviewed in a series of 40 minute chunks during his occasional free periods. For my part, I have never felt I was getting the best from such interviews in terms of in-depth reflection from the teachers. They were always in demand from other staff and pupils which often fragmented the interviews so that any sense of continuity was lost. Similarly, such interviews were clearly conducted in a work environment which itself can shape the nature of the interactions. In view of all this, I usually prefer to interview teachers in their own home. Symbolically this is important. It is definitely **their** terrain, **their** territory, that you as an outsider are invited into. While teachers may still be short of time in their private lives I have found that they relax much more in their homes, talk more freely about themselves, and generally reflect upon their life at a deeper level.

The life history interviews I conduct are best described as 'reflexive' (Hammersley and Atkinson, 1983) and do not have a rigid structure. This does not mean there is no structure at all. There most certainly is, and I usually enter the interview with some key themes that I wish to touch upon during the course of it. For example, the influence of the family in early life, experiences in school, the decision to become a PE teacher, and the influence of significant others in their lives. These themes, and others, derive from my previous contacts with PE teachers, my own experiences as a physical educator, and my previous research into this subject area. Later interviews often focus upon issues raised by the teacher in previous interviews or they followed new lines of development initiated by both the teacher and myself. Importantly, throughout the process my own experiences were often shared as part of the on-going dialogue in what Woods (1985, p. 13) has called a 'mutual endeavour', a 'conversation with a purpose'. As Corradi (1991) comments:

> There is the fact that the narrative is engendered by a question on the part of the researcher, and it takes shape in a dialogue that places narrator and researcher on an equal footing. In fact, very soon after the beginning of the interview there will no longer be a questioner and an answerer, one who understands and one who is understood. Instead each of the participants is understood by the other and altered by the interaction with each other. This face-to-face relationship directs the life story and makes it the product of an intersubjective process of knowledge. The life story contains the narrator and the researcher; through dialogue the latter becomes a constituent element of his or her own object of study. (p. 108).

The flow of the interview, its direction and pace were predominantly controlled by the teachers themselves. For me, this issue of control was important. My choice to focus upon the lives of teachers, rather than directly upon their practice in the classroom, gave much greater control to the teachers. In relation to this, Goodson (1991b) has expressed concern over those who wish to develop collaborative modes of research that give full equality and stature to the teacher but who then focus upon the practice of teachers as the initial and predominant focus. He argues that for the researcher this focus may seem quite unproblematic. However, for the teacher it may seem to be the maximum point of vulnerability. For Goodson a more valuable and less vulnerable entry point would be to examine teachers' work in the context of their lives since this focus potentially allows the teacher greater authority and control over the research process.

> *Talking about her or his own life the teacher is, in this specific sense, in a less immediately exposed situation; and the 'exposure' can be more carefully, consciously and personally controlled. (This is not, it should be noted, to argue that once again 'exploitation' might not take place, nor that there are no longer major ethical questions to do with exposure.) But I think this starting point has substantive as well as strategic advantages. (Goodson, 1991b, p. 148).*

Where possible other sources of data, such as written documents were incorporated to supplement the life stories and to provide further insights into the life history of the individual. Once again the availability of such documents was controlled by the teacher. These various data sources are informing a study that is still on-going so the following is based on a provisional analysis of the data so far regarding the life histories of PE teachers in England. This provisional analysis has raised my awareness of the multidimensional nature of marginality and the impact it can have for those who work as PE teachers in schools. Consequently, the data that follows has been selected with a view to fleshing out several of these dimensions and this selection needs to be recognised as I attempt to move beyond the consciousness of individuals to locate their voices in the wider socio-historic landscape that they inhabit. In doing so I hope to illustrate the potential of the life history approach to illuminate both our understanding of individual lives and the manner in which these are intimately related to and shaped by the lives of others in society.

DIMENSION 1: SUBJECT STATUS AND SINGULAR MARGINALITY

Various scholars, such as Hoyle (1986), have commented on the status problem that is associated with the subject of PE in schools. He noted, 'What one suspects is that physical education is universally lower rather than higher in the pecking order of school subjects' (p. 43). While status itself is a multifaceted concept there was an awareness across generations among those interviewed that physical educators had a poor anti-intellectual and non-academic image (also see Sparkes et al, 1990).

I mean everybody is moaning about the lack of time because of the National Curriculum. But it's systematically been taken away from us [the PE department] over the last five years. We're down to three hours a fortnight for the first-years. That was something like five periods just five years ago......It's low status as regards PE in the school. It's an area that just gets taken from, as does music, and art and drama. We are all shoved into one faculty, the Faculty of Performing Arts. It makes me feel resentful....The head of PE, he's resentful. He's always pushing all the time to get more of a profile for PE.....just to get more recognition....the fact that what we are contributing to the curriculum is something worthwhile. It's not just a time filler.....In terms of PE they just see me as somebody who does a lot of sport.....They don't see us as intellectuals...I don't think anybody does it deliberately but a lot of the time I feel like I'm being patted on the head and put in the corner.......Going into the staff room on my maths days they sort of say 'Oh, you've got your maths hat on', and they don't talk about PE things like house matches. I'm addressed as a normal human being. (Female, first year teacher)

It annoys me that I see subjects that are afforded status because of certain qualifications. Like people say 'Oh, he's an English teacher'. The fact is that he is afforded status because English is seen as a priority subject, purely because he's an English teacher - nothing about what he brings to the subject.....It just niggles me. You get the impression of people, because they are dealing in what everyone recognises as an academic subject, that what they are bringing to it is better than what I am bringing to PE, purely by virtue of the qualification and course I followed. But because it's academic, I mean in the National Curriculum you get English, Maths and Science [core subjects]. It's good that PE is in there obviously [as a foundation subject] but it's afforded less of a status because it's not an academic subject. That's the impression I get. (Male, early career).

Physical educators from different generations were also aware that other staff did not see theirs as an important subject. A 46 year old late-career PE teacher made the following comments based on her experiences at the grammar [selective entry by examination] school she first taught in during the mid 1960s and the comprehensive school [non-selective entry] she was teaching in at the end of the 1980s.

> *In some ways it could have been described in the grammar school days as an awful job because the status of PE was so low anyway. I was only one of about four non-graduates on a very academic staff and such people actually sort of regarded you as an inferior being..... PE as a whole had a bad name in the school. We were rather tolerated.....The important thing was 'O' levels and it [PE] was useful because they let off steam....I mean we had a very good name for modern languages. Now some of them actually did three and that came out of PE time.*

> *[In the comprehensive school] It's a bit of a joke. We're useful for controlling less able kids. Until next year the less able kids in the lower part of the school get more PE than the others.....They think it is good for them to let off steam.....they're sort of more worn out and a bit more manageable. And the fact that we are filling up the timetable. But as far as making any serious contribution it's not deemed important..... And I'm quite sure that the ways things are going that our head does not see the need to have a head of a PE department who can do anything in the way of curriculum development - just keep the kids happy and keep winning the matches.......Basically the status of PE is a joke.... that's one of the very difficult things when you are trying to get out [leave the subject area of PE and teach another subject] - you are regarded as 'all brawn and no brains'. People make generalizations and you have to work really hard to dispel them.*

Others who continued to teach PE throughout their career in school but have now retired also recall similar indicators of marginality. It would seem that for both male and female PE teachers across generations working in a variety of schools that their subject is seen as less important than others. On those occasions where it is granted some esteem it is for reasons that are questionable; for example, providing a form of catharsis to tire less able or difficult to manage students and make them more placid and controllable during classroom lessons.

STRUCTURED IMPLICATIONS OF LOW STATUS

The personal troubles described by these physical educators have not been constructed in a vacuum. They are located within a broader social, political and economic context that has deep historical roots. While a more thorough review of these roots and their impact upon contemporary concerns is available elsewhere (see Mangan, 1981; Mangan & Park, 1987; Sparkes & Templin, 1992; Sparkes, Templin & Schempp, 1990), it is worth mentioning here that relationship of the mind to the body has been a source of debate throughout recorded history. For example, the ancient Greeks assumed that the physical and mental aspects of the whole being formed two distinct entities, with the former in the service of the latter. The Romans believed that a healthy body was indispensable to the maintenance of a healthy mind, while Descartes in the 17th century confirmed the mind-body split in a way that gave privileged status to the mind as the definition of the person, and an underprivileged status to the body which was conceptualised simply as a machine.

These beliefs have permeated Western thought and have shaped educational theory and practice in such a way that propositional knowledge, of the know-that kind, is regarded as something apart from and superior to procedural knowledge of the know-how kind. Therefore, a mental-manual dichotomy is reinforced, leisure is seen as subsidiary to work, and play is regarded as inferior to work. Commenting on this Giroux (1983) argues that one of the dominant features of the school is the manner in which it recognises and rewards mental labour while at the same time denigrating manual labour. Likewise, Evans and Williams (1989) point out that 'Teachers in schools, like society at large, tend to celebrate and reward general knowledge work rather than technical knowledge, the work of the mind rather than the work of the hand and the body' (p. 247).

Children are made aware of this status differential very early on in their school careers as a study by Apple (1979) of entry into a junior school illustrated. His work revealed that one of the first lessons they were taught was that in school there were 'work things' and 'play things'. 'Work things' included books, paper, writing instruments and the like. 'Play things' included balls of all sorts, jump ropes and bean bags, etc. That is, all the objects found in a typical PE class were classified as 'play things'. A second lesson the children learned was that one never played with 'work things' and one never worked with 'play things'. The children were also taught that play was appropriate only after the work had been completed. This reinforced the message that work is more important than play. As such, the hidden curriculum of the formal curriculum transmitted the powerful and disturbing message that the very concept of ability is intimately linked to the intellectual-cognitive domain. These assumptions, messages and practices have serious implications for the subject area of PE, whose curricula draw upon a range of play-like physical activities, such as sports, games and health-related exercises.

Physical education, and subjects like art, music and drama are engaged in teaching a particular bodily skill or set of skills. As a consequence, they find difficulty gaining acceptance within what Connell (1985) describes as the 'hegemonic academic curriculum' that is devoted to self-referring, abstract bodies of knowledge. He suggests that this form of curriculum 'has pride of place in the schools, it dominates most people's ideas of what real learning is about; its logic has the most powerful influence on the organisation of the school, and of the education system generally; and it is able to marginalise and subordinate the other curricula that are present' (p. 87). The continuing marginalisation of these curricula manifests itself in the low status and prestige given to them in schools, which in turn influences their positioning in relation to the allocation of power, resources and funding between subject areas. Therefore, the experiences of marginality and subordination expressed earlier by the PE teachers are located in a wider web of constraints that shapes their lives and career opportunities in schools.

How others think and feel about a subject has important implications for those who teach it. Such perceptions interact in subtle ways to structure career opportunities and development in a marginal subject that are, for the most part, beyond the control of the individual. For example, it is generally assumed that the so-called academic subjects, which are taken to contain within their boundaries some form of examinable knowledge, are more suitable for the 'able' students, while other subjects are not. More resources are given to able students and hence to the academic subjects. Therefore, as Goodson (1984) reminds us, the conflict over the status of examinable knowledge is above all a battle over the material resources and career prospects available to each subject community or subject teacher. In its simplest form, the higher the status of the subject the better the prospect for the teachers involved with regard to staffing ratios, higher salaries, more graded posts and better career prospects. Consequently, status means strength and strength means greater bargaining power for the finite resources available within the individual school and the educational system as a whole. Pollard (1982) notes how these finite resources set parameters for activities in the school and the manner in which these are dependent 'on the particular policies or patterns of allocation which exist in each school. These will reflect the institutional bias, in particular the influence of the headteacher, and the relative power and negotiating skills of the staff as they bid for resources' (p. 32). In relation to these issues the following comments from PE teachers are illuminating.

> *I think that probably teachers in the academic subjects have an easier time in getting incentive allowances....I don't know, it's just an impression I get....So in a sense it's more difficult for you to get on if you are a PE teacher. If you are in competition with other subjects then it is more difficult. There are accepted routes for promotion for PE people in that you go off into the pastoral system......But against promotion against teachers in other subjects I think we have got a more difficult job. I mean it is a competition now with LMS - you've definitely got a more difficult job. (Male, early career)*

> *I think the major thing [the lack of promotion] it's all based on, I think she [the headteacher] doesn't rate PE. I'll emphasise that again - we needn't bother being there. If she had her way I think that PE would be removed from the timetable. She sees PE as just a complete and utter waste of time. That's how she views it. You can't get on in this school if you are PE. As a PE teacher I'm wasting me time. Sally's [female member of PE department] wasting her time, and everyone else is wasting their time. (Male, early career).*

What these comments connect each individual to are patterns of disadvantage that operate within the educational system and the wider society. For example, figures provided by the Department of Education and Science (1982), analysing teachers qualified in each subject by salary scale, indicate that PE teachers have a lot less chance than those in other subjects to rise above the level of a scale 3 position within their subject department. Commenting upon their findings, the DES remark 'Nevertheless there are marked differences between subjects, with physical education, art/craft, craft, design and technology, home economics and music having a lower proportion of senior posts and scale 4 posts than the more 'academic' subjects' (p. 3). Apparently, those who choose to teach the more practical subjects are unable to compete with other subjects and are destined to remain on the lower rungs of the managerial ladder.

Historically, Ball (1987) reminds us, certain patterns of structural advantage and disadvantage have been institutionalised in our schools. He argues that these ingrained career patterns extend across schools and that 'The most significant of these structures is the organisation and differential status of subject departments' (p. 174). More recently, Evans & Williams (1989) emphasise this point and note 'Teachers' careers are structured (limited or facilitated) by ideologies in the school work place that influence and differently define the position and status of both men and women and the academic and the "non-academic" (practical) curriculum; and that these ideologies have their bases in wider society' (p. 237). They go on to argue that competition between subject groups and individuals is a fundamental feature of school life and an inescapable aspect of individual advancement through teaching. However, they point out that the competition is not equal in that teachers do not have the same status, social, or professional resources on which to base their claims.

DIMENSION 2: A WOMAN'S EXPERIENCE OF DOUBLE MARGINALITY

Choosing to teach a practical subject brings the problems associated with marginality to all those who make such a choice. However, the problems and dilemmas associated with marginality are not experienced by all PE teachers in the same way. That is, subject status alone does not account for the many difficulties that some teachers experience when they attempt to gain promotion or look for a job. Acker (1989) emphasises that teachers need to be seen as a heterogeneous group.

> *For those belonging to particular groups there are blockages and barriers making their passage more difficult. Individuals possess different currencies (qualifications, length and type of experience, subject specialities) but their probabilities of holding these also depend on their class, sex, race, age and other identifications and memberships. Even qualities like motivation and personality may be differently received and interpreted by others according to who displays them. (p. 19).*

In this sense, Ball (1987) argues, 'Women teachers may validly be regarded as a distinct interest group within the school if only because the overall pattern of their career development is so clearly different from that of men teachers.......Women are severely disadvantaged in career terms by the male dominance of schools' (p. 191). For example, drawing upon survey data of career patterns of PE teachers in a county in England, Evans and Williams (1989) found that some striking patterns of inequality merged between men and women when the distribution of responsibilities, rewards, and status were examined. These differences, they suggest, have much to do with the fact that 'the language and structure of schooling and the subject departments inside them are often deeply shaped by patriarchy. The gatekeepers to jobs are predominantly men and they do not always believe women are either capable or suitable, because of their competing family and work roles, for advancement into senior positions' (p. 238).

Similar disparities pervade the educational system as contributors to edited volumes by Acker (1989) and De Lyon & Migniuolo (1989) indicate. Both draw upon qualitative and quantitative data to illustrate that while the teaching profession is dominated in the numerical sense by women, the positions of real power remain the domain of men. The dynamics and complexities of the processes that socially construct and maintain such inequalities are beyond the scope of this monograph to discuss. However, in relation to this process the following draws upon some strands of one PE teacher's life history to indicate how this approach can illuminate, and help to explain, the dilemmas that many women face in the context of a patriarchal system.

Jenny is now in her early 50s and has recently left the teaching profession having accepted early retirement along with a redundancy payment in a school with falling enrolment. Looking back, Jenny remembers being an active and committed young PE teacher at a school in London during the late 1950s. Sharing a flat with friends, spending long hours after school running school teams, and still finding time for her own sporting activities. During this period Jenny went for a holiday in the West of England where she met her future husband who worked in that area. They got married at the start of the 1960s and, in keeping with many married women who end up teaching in the areas where their husbands are employed, Jenny moved away from London to be with her husband.

Having gained temporary teaching positions for a while she gained full-time employment as a PE teacher in a secondary school. At this stage of her life Jenny loved teaching and felt as though she wanted a career and 'get on' in teaching. Jenny did become departmental head towards the end of the 1970s but a range of events acted to disillusion her and make her happy to leave teaching in 1987. However, in terms of her career progression several points are noticeable that revolve around marriage and children. Talking about her marriage which ended in divorce Jenny notes:

> *The getting married in the first place was a key point that changed my life [laughs]. By picking a wrong marriage.... We just weren't compatible at all.....Being a PE teacher didn't fit in with being married. He objected to the Saturday morning business and the after school clubs.....He didn't think much of me earning more than he did....The reasons for it all [the divorce]....I think it was because he wasn't as well educated as I was and he couldn't accept it. He couldn't accept that I was getting on in my job, especially when I was made head of department in the 70s.....I think that was the way it was in those days, that men were in charge......The time I gave to PE created tensions. He would say 'You spend more time at school than you do at home'. It got to the stage when he began to say 'But you're not really doing all this sort of thing. It wasn't all work'. Hinting at some affair. He'd just got hang-ups about it. He knew he was marrying a PE teacher but whether he knew what was entailed I don't know. I don't know if he realised how much out of school time is involved in PE. He certainly couldn't accept it.*

In 1963 Jenny had her first child. Four years later her second child was born and 18 months after this came her third. With the divorce in 1974 Jenny gained custody of the three children. She notes, 'The divorce was a major upheaval in my life....I have basically brought up the three kids by myself. That obviously has affected my life in a pretty big way'. Jenny felt that her choice to have children, regardless of the divorce, had a dramatic impact upon her career aspirations because it meant her being out of full-time teaching for six years.

> *In those days you just had to leave and that was the end of your job. You had to apply for another job if you wanted to go back...It was a big factor for women and their jobs and their careers.....there had never been any choice so you just accepted it.....it was unfair especially if you were a woman. It affects your career. Not only that it affects you later on in life as well. I would probably have had a bigger pension. I would have had a bigger redundancy payment, but time out for three kids reduces all that doesn't it.*

Having had her children Jenny returned to teaching, picking up part-time employment, until she managed to get a full-time post that eventually led to her being promoted to departmental head. However, she recognises that this came about more by luck than judgment 'But it was all luck. You can't plan if you have kids. It's different trying to have a career if you are a woman.....Women don't tend to get to the top do they. I don't understand it'. Bringing up her three children by herself after the divorce was also a major factor in the shaping of Jenny's career aspirations as she coped with being a single parent attempting to bring some stability into their lives 'Once I was divorced I had to concentrate quite a bit of time on the kids.....I suppose that's why my career came to a halt at that stage because I was thinking about them mainly rather than myself.....If I hadn't had the kids to worry about and think what was best for them, I could probably have moved to somewhere different'. While a range of tensions runs through her life history, Jenny sums up her situation in the following way, 'I suppose I had to lead two separate lives'.

CONTEXTUALISING A GENDERED CAREER

Jenny, as a mother and a PE teacher, is not alone in attempting to lead two separate lives as a means of coping with the role conflicts that arise when individuals are faced with simultaneous, yet contradictory, sets of expectations from self and others. Many women experience the tensions and strains, both physical and mental, of running a home, trying to be a good mother, and trying to be a good teacher. Acker (1990) talks of women 'who juggled domestic and work commitments with the finely honed skills of circus performers' (p. 18). Indeed, Spencer (1986) talks of women teachers having a "triple day" of work 'They taught all day, did most of the housework (including child care), and then did more school work, such as grading papers' (p. 13).

It has been argued elsewhere (Sparkes & Templin, 1992) that performing these multiple roles often has important implications for how women are perceived in schools and concomitantly for their occupational careers. Furthermore, these dual pressures act in important ways to shape the expectations and perceptions that women have about themselves that have consequences for the way they function as people both in and out of school. As Connell (1985) argued 'the way one responds to the emotional demands of teaching becomes decisive for one's whole emotional economy' (p. 151). While many teachers would like to compartmentalise their life at home and school it remains impossible for most to do so since relationships in one facet of a teacher's life are interrelated to relationships in other areas. According to Spencer (1986) in her study of contemporary women teachers, 'Home and school events were ever-present realities, regardless of differing situational contexts.....Dissatisfaction with teaching influenced personal and marital relations, and personal problems influenced teaching effectiveness. The effects of home and school were inextricably interrelated, (pp. 185-186).

Women in other walks of life also experience a range of contradictions between being a mother and maintaining some form of independence in the outside world and their experiences are connected to those of Jenny. For example, Ball (1987, pp. 198-199) commented 'Negotiations over the issue of female labour will be resolved differently in different households according to whether tradition (patriarchy) or rationality (maximization of economic interests) prevail'. He goes on to argue that where both models have equal or similar importance for household members in explaining their social world that negotiations are likely to lead to conflict 'The costs arising from such a conflict may be high; working wives may find that they face difficult decisions in weighing up their marriage and family against their career'. At times this can lead to breakdowns in the marital relationship. However, even where resolutions within the household are achieved, he emphasises 'the organisation of family life alongside work life may prove problematic.....the contemporary conditions of employment continue to be orientated to the male employee. Married women find they must adapt themselves to the conditions based upon a male norm'. As Cunnison (1985, p. 32), cited in Ball (1987), bluntly puts it 'The world of work is made-to-measure for men who do not get pregnant and have family responsibilities'.

Of course, I do not wish to suggest that all women, whether single, married, living with partners, or divorced, experience teaching in the same way as Jenny. Women in similar situations may have very different stories to tell. Stories will also vary for those in different situations. The availability of other stories, however, does not detract from the importance of the one told by Jenny as it helps to illuminate and explain the strands of oppression that structured her life chances and experiences along with those of many other women. This exposure can assist in the on-going critique of the dominant structures in our society that has been mounted by feminist scholars in recent years. In this sense, exploring the life histories of women (and other oppressed groups) provides a powerful form of engagement that is able to widen women's awareness about the structural realities of their lives that would include the ways in which the socialising process conditions them to accept masculinised images of schooling, accept/tolerate discrimination and to undervalue themselves in teaching. Furthermore, their stories invariably raise issues regarding the part that men (and other women) play in creating and maintaining oppressive relationships that need to be challenged and transformed.

DIMENSION 3: SEXUAL IDENTITY AND TRIPLE MARGINALITY

While lives are gendered in teaching there is another powerful dimension relating to marginality that too often remains unspoken. Few studies have focused on the experiences of lesbian and gay teachers. This has led Squirrell (1989a) to comment, 'Within mainstream academic research it would appear that sexuality and education are not thought a suitable coupling' (p. 87). Notable exceptions include the work of Griffin (1991, 1992a), Olsen (1987) and Squirrell (1989a, 1989b) who have drawn upon interview data to highlight the management identity strategies that lesbian and gay teachers are forced to adopt in a cultural climate characterised by homophobia and heterosexism. Within the literature, studies that have specifically considered the experiences of lesbian and gay PE teachers in schools are even harder to find. There are rare exceptions and the phenomenological investigations informed by oppression theory of Woods (1992) reveal how homophobia, heterosexism and sexism envelop the world of lesbian PE teachers in the USA. On the experiences of gay PE teachers in schools there is nothing and a deafening silence prevails. Bearing this in mind, the following focuses upon a lesbian physical educator, called Jessica [a pseudonym], who has recently begun teaching at a secondary school in England.

> *People don't have a positive image of a gay person at all. There are no positive role models. All the stereotypes tend to be negative.........I feel invisible on a lot of counts actually. I feel invisible sure, in terms of what I basically am in terms of my sexuality. I also feel invisible in as much that I haven't been able to make the contacts, either socially or professionally, that would give people a rounded idea of me.*

The identity management strategies utilised by Jessica during various phases of her life to protect her substantial sense of self in different contexts characterised by varying degrees of homophobia and heterosexism are focused upon in detail elsewhere (see Sparkes, 1994 a, Sparkes & Tiihonen, 1992). Similarly, the ethical and political dimensions of collaborative research as a form of solidarity between a lesbian teacher and a heterosexual researcher are commented upon elsewhere (see Sparkes, 1994 b). Consequently, for the purposes of this monograph, I will concentrate briefly upon some of Jessica's experiences in her school and how she is rendered both silent and invisible due to her sexual identity.

Currently, Jessica is forced to lead a 'double life' in which her professional and social life are fragmented and distanced from one another. In describing a typical week she comments:

> *The weekend of it I'm in London with my friends. That's kind of almost reinforcing this need to get out of one life and into another because I'm geographically picking myself up and moving. Spending time with different people at the weekends and having a social life with my friends. Then back home it's back here....That's reinforcing that split........It's a conscious decision. I feel I almost need it. I need to be able to relax, to be me.*

Towards the latter part of her first year in teaching Jessica 'came out', that is, explicitly disclosed her lesbian identity, to another female teacher in the school. This incident highlights the sense of isolation and loneliness that Jessica was experiencing and the need she felt for at least the support of one colleague that she could relax with in a professional context.

> *I came out to her. I was actually quite conscious of the burden, of relief, a sensation of "at least I've told one person". I mean, one is so many more than none. Sadly enough she's now left the school and she's got another job somewhere else. So I'm back to square one in those terms......you see Alison [a pseudonym] was really the only person that I'd spoken to socially, that I would talk about my life outside of school to.....Just that there was somebody else on the staff that knew. I think it was almost, at least somebody else knows, at least somebody could be on my side if anything was to happen.*

These 'happenings' included a fear of discrimination from colleagues, pupils and parents along with an awareness that this might lead to her eventual dismissal from her teaching post. As Jessica commented when asked what the reactions of parents might be if they knew she was a lesbian, "It just doesn't bear thinking about".

Informal conversations with teaching colleagues, several of whom who expressed homophobic views, made Jessica far from convinced that she could count on their support in the event of her sexual identity becoming public knowledge. For example, during a social evening with a group of new teachers in the school one of them told Jessica about her honeymoon in Florida.

We were talking loads in the pub. She was like, 'We went to Key West. We didn't like the place, there were gay people everywhere. I don't know why, it was just horrible'. I just sat there and thought, 'Um' (laughs). I'd had the best time of my life in Key West and I lived there for eight months and then another six, and I loved it for just those reasons and it just felt weird....I said, 'Oh, I've spent some time there. I found it quite interesting. Perhaps it's changed'. I don't know, I said something stupid.

Such conversations confirmed Jessica's view that the teaching profession had a negative view of lesbian women and gay men and that there was, 'Still a lot of fear, derision and prejudice. There are still a lot of people I think who hold the views that anybody of a different sexual orientation is a child molester, which is totally laughable.......There are a lot of dangerous myths still around and still in teaching, maybe more than other areas of work because we're dealing with children'.

These concerns, coupled with the fact that the one person she had explicitly come out to and looked to for support had left the school, acted to literally silence Jessica on several occasions. For example, an in-service day during her second year of teaching highlighted the tensions of having to constantly suppress her substantial sense of self and beliefs in the school context. Part of the day focused on the counselling role of the teacher when dealing with sensitive issues in the classroom. During seminar sessions child abuse and sexual abuse were mentioned. Jessica wanted to raise the issue of sexual identity as a relevant topic, but didn't. She remembers:

I was aware, I was tense the whole time thinking, 'I want to say something. This issue needs to be raised'. But I just didn't feel I could do it. I felt that as soon as I stood up and opened my mouth that I would either just reinforce what people thought already or suspected, or it would just be incriminating myself. I just couldn't get that thought out of my mind..... I just felt the incrimination so much I couldn't do it. I was thinking on the way here this morning, If there had been one other person, who I had come out to before, I'd have built up a relationship with her by now to have actually said to her at coffee break, 'Mention this', and she would have done because she wouldn't have feared that because it wouldn't have been the same kind of issue for her............I just felt horrible. I felt like a coward and I'd let myself down. I felt really strongly about it. I got home in a hell of a mood. I just felt like, Here's me sort of purporting all this stuff about bringing the issue out in other ways, and when I get the chance to professionally, I don't do it......I really feel so isolated.... I didn't have the confidence because I didn't know what the reaction would be.

44

In combination, the daily self denial coupled with the on-going dislocation and forced separation of her professional and personal life are exacting a heavy emotional toll on Jessica. She is keenly aware that for her to approximate her ideals will require a change of job in the immediate future in the hope of finding greater integration of self and situation.

CONTEXTUALISING SILENCE & INVISIBILITY: THE PRIVATE-PUBLIC DIVIDE

Clearly, the brief glimpses of moments from Jessica's story indicate that there is a third dimension of marginality operating in the lives of teachers in general, and PE teachers in particular, with regard to issues of sexual identity. Her experiences of oppression are historically embedded in the stereotypical views held about women who are involved in PE and sport. In relation to this Griffin (1992b) has outlined the socially constructed early 20th-century origins of the lesbian stereotype along with the political functions that homophobia achieves in a sexist and heterosexist culture, such as conferring privilege and normalcy on particular social groups - men and heterosexuals. In a similar vein, Woods (1992) argues that while all lesbian and gay teachers are targets of homophobia, those who teach subjects that are not consistent with traditional gender roles are particularly vulnerable to homophobic accusations.

> *The lesbian physical educator is perhaps the most vulnerable target of all. She (and all other female physical educators) is frequently assumed to be lesbian whether or not she publicly discloses her sexual orientation......Within the firmly entrenched male domain of sport and physical education there is an assumed relationship between traditional gender roles and sexuality.....To put it more simply, to be athletic is to be equated with masculinity and masculine women are labelled as lesbian. Therefore, athletic women are stereotyped as lesbian......Allegations of lesbianism are used to intimidate and harass women in physical education and sport. (p. 91).*

Likewise, Lenskyj (1991) pointed out that, 'There is ample evidence of the chilly climate confronting lesbians in sport and physical education contexts..........Lesbians whose work involves school age children - for example coaches and physical education teachers - are particularly vulnerable to homophobia' (pp. 62-63). Due to this vulnerability and the threat of being labelled a lesbian as a constant source of intimidation, homophobia affects and constrains the lives of all women physical educators both lesbian and heterosexual, reducing their ability to challenge the status quo. The structural constraints imposed upon the life of Jessica with regard to homophobia, heterosexism and sexism indicate how these dynamically interconnected strands of oppression operate to shape her daily experiences. Manifestations of this influence are evident in Jessica's continued silence and invisibility in school. In relation to this Griffin and Genasci (1990) comment, 'Because of the extreme negative stigma attached to homosexuality in our culture, many, perhaps most, gay and lesbian people live double lives and are invisible members of our schools and communities' (p. 212).

Jessica's silence and invisibility, and the identity management strategies she is forced to adopt (both in and out of schools), are further structured by heterosexual hegemony that for Burrell & Hearn (1989), 'tends to construct lesbians and gay men as isolated exceptions, so that they and their sexuality come to be seen, by many heterosexuals, at least, as private and individual, even as personal "problems"' (p. 23). To highlight this issue I want to focus on the strategy that Jessica has adopted to protect her substantial sense of self which involves maintaining a split between her public (work) life and her private (personal) life. This strategy is evident in the study by Woods (1992) who worked with North American lesbian PE teachers.

> *The participants justified their personal/professional split in many ways, describing it as a norm for all teachers, as an individual right, as a necessity, or as a given for lesbians. All experienced conflict around separating their lesbian identity from their teacher identity. This conflict took the form of both resentment and fear: resentment because there was no overlap between their two worlds, and fear because there was. Many of the participants described making this separation as a choice, but in various ways, their words and experiences contradicted this description. As lesbians, they believed disclosure of their sexual orientation would cost them their jobs, and as female physical educators, they assumed they were already stereotyped as lesbians. Both these assumptions shaped the way they experienced being a lesbian physical educator. From their perspective, the only real choices were to conceal their sexual orientation to stay in teaching or to leave teaching altogether. (p. 102).*

The strategy of splitting the private and public, the personal and the professional has been seen to operate in the lives of other lesbian and gay male subject teachers in schools (Squirrell, 1989a & b), and lesbians operating in other forms of organisation (Hall, 1989). Of course, this is not to suggest that heterosexual teachers do not draw upon this and a range of other coping strategies (Nias, 1989; Pollard, 1982). However, due to their positioning as heterosexuals their

46

experiences of this private/public split differ dramatically from those of Jessica. Equally, the *consequences*, as described earlier, of not rigorously maintaining this split are very different for lesbian and gay teachers when compared to their heterosexual colleagues. For example, one likely consequence of not maintaining this split for lesbian and gay teachers is that they would face discrimination on the basis of their sexual identity in applying for, or gaining promotion, within schools. Therefore, paradoxically, while the private/public split offers a form of protection against discrimination it also obscures the inequities experienced by lesbian and gay teachers in the public sphere of the school.

Jessica's identity management strategy is framed within the 'professional' expectation held by many of her colleagues that one's private home life should be kept separate from one's public work life. In particular, issues of sexual identity are commonly assumed to be 'private' affairs that should not be brought into the public and professional world of work. This view is informed by a liberal humanist ideology that Kitzinger (1987) suggests is a fundamental faith for many middle-class Western intellectuals that is rarely recognised as such, and rarely questioned in terms of how this value system can 'serve the interests of patriarchy in ensuring the continuing oppression of women' (p. 192). However, Kitzinger, and others (see Hearn, 1987; Khayatt, 1992; Walby, 1989) have revealed the deceptiveness of this distinction between public and private spheres and how, in fact, this dualism is very much rooted in the ideology of patriarchy and the key sets of patriarchal practices that relate to compulsory heterosexuality. As Bensimon (1992) argues, the private/public distinction is partial, distorting, and perverse.

> It is *partial* because.......the public/private distinction is derived from a vision of the public that takes into account only the reality of the dominant sexual class. It is *distorting* because......it normalizes sexuality as heterosexuality. And it is *perverse*, because......the public/private distinction provides a distinction for not bringing about change. (I use the term perverse to convey the terrible wrong that is committed when an argument is based on a logic that has the capacity of making an oppressive situation appear rational). (p. 99).

The work of Shilling (1991) on the spatial dimensions of social interaction and reproduction in schools is extremely useful in highlighting the partial and distorting nature of the private/ public divide. For Shilling, space is no longer seen just as an environment in which interaction takes place, but is taken to be deeply implicated in the production of individual identities and social inequalities, 'All social interaction takes place in space and it is impossible to conceive of social life outside of spatial contexts......Space does not just provide opportunities for people

47

to act, though, it also constrains the possibilities of individual action, (pp. 23-25). Drawing on Giddens' (1984) theory of *structuration*, Shilling focuses attention on the concepts of 'locale' and 'regionalisation' to illustrate how social space is implicated in the production of gender inequalities in schools, Shilling draws upon a number of ethnographic studies to illuminate how both front and back regions in schools are framed by patriarchal structures that provide rules and resources which men and women draw upon and have to take account of in their daily lives. In particular, he points to the staffroom as a gendered locale and challenges the common assumption that this social space in schools is a back region for teachers where they can 'escape' from pupils, drop the roles they play in teaching situations (front regions), make jokes about pupils, share information and news, socialise and repair their professional identities. In reviewing various studies on the general organisation of staffrooms and the forms of humour and joking that operate within them, Shilling comments:

> *This locale is also regionalised on the basis of gender and while the staffroom may be a 'haven' for some, it is also used as an area where male teachers exert their dominance over women.......Consequently, while the staffroom may be a place for men to relax, unwind, and escape from the pressures of classroom teaching, it may not offer the same benefits to many women. Furthermore, men not only draw on patriarchal cultural rules (i.e. sexist humour) to exert control over women in the specific locale of the staffroom. They may also organise resources within the staffroom itself to symbolically reflect their position of dominance.......The patriarchal cultural rules and resources drawn upon by male teachers make this part of the school an area embedded with different meanings for women and men. ....the staffroom may simply constitute a distinct set of pressures for women faced with male adults, rather than male pupils, attempting to exercise dominance and re-produce this locale as a male terrain. (pp. 38-39).*

The patriarchal cultural rules and resources that shape interactions in the staffroom are also laden with different meanings for lesbian teachers who experience further inequalities associated with their sexual identity in this locale. For Jessica, the staffroom and other supposed back regions such as staff socials, and informal gatherings in the pub are certainly not places where she can relax, repair her sense of identity, and disclose aspects of her self. Indeed, in these 'back' regions for others Jessica is in a 'front' situation where she is 'on guard' and has to deny and enclose her sense of self and identity in ways that can cause emotional stress and damage rather than bring about emotional repair. Therefore, while heterosexual women and men may be able to openly disclose aspects of themselves and their lives to others if they so choose in terms of, for example, mentioning what they did over the weekend with their husbands/wives/partners or families, this option is not available to Jessica who, feeling constantly under surveillance and being conscious of constant assessment from the vantage point of heterosexuality, carefully edits any conversation with other teachers, even in back regions, so as not to reveal her lesbian identity. As Khayatt (1992) comments:

> *What this means in the everyday life of a lesbian teacher is that she may not take her lover to staff functions, may not wear a ring or labrys or give any indication of her sexuality. She cannot talk openly about her weekend activities - in short, her life must remain invisible. This is in contrast to her heterosexual sister, who notes her attachment to a man by wearing a wedding (or engagement) band, who is encouraged to talk endlessly about her relationship, and whose pregnancy is celebrated as proof of his virility and her fertility. (p. 72).*

In the front regions when she is teaching and interacting with children, Jessica feels similar pressures. Therefore, in both front and back stage regions Jessica is denied an essential freedom which involves the freedom to interact in the public space without having to hide her sexual identity and construct her life in school according to the prescribed script of assumed heterosexuality (see Bensimon, 1992). This right is systematically granted to heterosexual teachers but systematically denied to Jessica in a way that legitimises the partial and distorting nature of the public/private dichotomy. Hall (1989) in her study of lesbians in organisations summarises the situation well.

> *Because the revelation of one's lesbianism could have serious consequences, these women were constantly preoccupied with concealing that aspect of their lives. Sometimes concealment occurred as automatically as retinal adjustment to light change. At other times, it was deliberate and felt more stressful. Whether automatic or deliberate, the process of concealment called for constant attention to every nuance of social interaction. The background buzz of assumptions became centrally important for the lesbian because it signalled where vigilance was necessary or where she could relax and 'be herself'. The workplace reality for the lesbian, therefore, was one of heightened awareness and sensitivity toward the usually hidden matrices of behaviour, values and attitudes in self and others. (p. 129).*

The partiality of the public/private dichotomy is further revealed when we consider how, for Jessica, these two spheres are not mutually exclusive but interactive. For example, the public sphere is able to significantly impact upon her private life in terms of where she spends her spare time with her partner. Similarly, Jessica's choice to live away from the catchment area of the school was informed by her concern to protect her lesbian identity from pupils, other teachers and parents. Even though Jessica lives close to a major city which she can 'escape' to, in terms of her concerns to guard against exposure there is a real sense of what Burrell and Hearn (1989) call institutional closure that, 'brings into play a particular, and sometimes very powerful, set of organizational controls over time and space, over sexual time and sexual bodies' (p. 22).

The distorting nature of the public/private dichotomy is also evident in the manner in which it reduces lesbianism to sexuality. Here, the common assumption is that being a lesbian is simply an issue of what a women wants to do in private and with whom. However, as the moments from Jessica's life reveal her lesbian identity is central to her very being as a person and shapes the way she relates to the world as a whole. Yet, in the ideologically heterosexual school environment her sexual identity is denied and her public life is dominated by a range of strategies that are designed to conceal from others what Jessica sees as the 'essence' of herself. Therefore, the pressures to keep her lesbianism a private and invisible matter forces Jessica to restrict her public interactions with both children and other teachers. That is, the private impacts upon the public.

Finally, Bensimon (1992) comments that the the public/private distinction is perverse, 'because it sets up a situation which, in effect delegitimises complaints about inequalities in the public sphere that arise from the personal choices one makes in and about the private sphere' (p. 107). Woods (1992) also comments on how defining sexual identity as a personal and private matter acts to deflect institutions from developing non-discrimination policies on the basis of sexual identity, 'When sexual orientation is viewed from this perspective, the institutional forces that shape and define oppression are not questioned......The onus of change is placed on the individual and not the system. One consequence of a person-change perspective is person-blame' (pp. 114-115). As such, this stance allows heterosexual teachers and administrators to appear liberal and tolerant with regard to lesbian and gay issues without having to recognise and address both the personalised, sociopolitical and institutionalised aspects of homophobia and heterosexism that renders many of their lesbian and gay colleagues invisible. Essentially, as Bensimon (1992) argues:

> The public/private distinction universalizes sexuality as heterosexuality, blinding those who belong to the dominant sexual class - women and men - to the very specific ways in which they impose invisible and intolerable existences on lesbian faculty. The invisibility of lesbian faculty is maintained by the public/ private distinction. (p. 101).

A BRIEF COMMENT ON LIFE HISTORIES AND MARGINAL TALES

Clearly, in the short space available I have not been able to do justice to either the descriptive or the explanatory power of life history research. However, I hope I have been able to provide indicators of each. On reading about the moments from the lives of PE teachers it is clear that marginality needs to be seen as a multidimensional phenomena that impacts upon the lives of people in very different ways depending upon their social positioning. This has vital importance if we wish to understand how teachers operate in schools and why they do the things they do. It is also vital if we wish to enhance the professional development of teachers throughout their careers.

Of course, some might argue that all the life histories of PE teachers will tell us about is the world of PE. However, this is a rather short-sighted and distorted view of how life histories can operate to challenge orthodox and mainstream views of teachers and teaching. As Goodson (1992b) has pointed out much truth resides in the margins and this truth reflects upon us all. As you read the words of the PE teachers earlier did you begin to see them in different ways? Did you begin to see yourself in relation to them in different ways? Did their words make you reflect about yourself, even though you might not be a PE teacher? If the answer is 'yes' then we can begin to see how life history work can impact on the lives of others. Here, the moments provided earlier from Jessica's life provide a good example. The presentation of such moments was not done with a view to being predictive or claiming that Jessica's experiences can be generalised to all lesbian teachers in schools, but rather to present a view of schooling from a particular standpoint that for the most part has been, and still is, repressed. Accordingly, how Jessica experiences educational institutions as a beginning teacher, how she relates these experiences to other moments in her life, and the strategies she adopts to cope with specific situations, provide important insights into a reality that is oppositional to the taken-for-granted reality of the dominant and privileged sexual class in schools, that is, heterosexuals. In commenting upon the benefits of adopting a lesbian standpoint Harding (1991) comments:

> In identifying what one can see with the help of a lesbian standpoint, I do not point exclusively to insights about lesbians. The standpoint epistemologies have a different logic. Just as the research and scholarship that begin from the standpoint of women more generally is not exclusively about women, so these insights are not exclusively about lesbians. The point is that starting from the (many different) daily activities of lesbians enables us to see things that might otherwise have been invisible to us, not just about those lives but about heterosexual women's lives and men's lives, straight as well as gay'. (p. 252).

Likewise, Bensimon (1992) recognises that while taking a lesbian standpoint is to situate knowledge in the particular experience of women who are lesbian in ways that reject the notion of women's experiences as universal regardless of sexual identity, race, age, or class, the knowledge produced is significantly not just about lesbians.

> Viewing the public sphere......from the lives of those in the margins expands the unidimensional and partial story of those situated in the center and provokes a different understanding of their own situation as well as of the situation they create for others......The lesbian standpoint is valuable because it has the capacity to reveal how the vision of the dominant heterosexual class structures the public sphere in ways that can be oppressive for lesbian faculty. The struggles lesbians wage in the process of constructing lives within a public space that is structured by the discourse of compulsory heterosexuality may be the source of a different vision of the academy. (p. 102).

By presenting the struggles that Jessica faces on a daily basis to construct her life and maintain her sense of self in the public spaces that the school provides my intention was to provide insights into how schooling as a patriarchal institution, that is ideologically and culturally heterosexual, creates and maintains a set of inequitable circumstances that exercise a level of control over the 'private' lives of lesbian teachers. My intention was also to illustrate how these circumstances lead these teachers to experience 'public' school life in ways that are hard to imagine for those (the majority) who are the beneficiaries of the privileges of heterosexuality. Finally, by focusing upon the enforced split Jessica has to make between her public (professional) and private (personal) lives I hope to indicate how Jessica's experiences as a lesbian PE teacher are structured and shaped by existing sets of social relationships that are oppressive.

Equally, presenting moments from the lives of other teachers can fracture our taken-for-granted views and lead us to engage in some serious rethinking about ourselves and others as teachers. This in itself, for me at least, is justification enough for conducting life history research.

EXPLORING LIVES - SOME ETHICAL ISSUES

As you read through the previous sections on marginality you may have wondered what my relationship was with those I interviewed. In the last five years I have explored the life histories of many PE teachers and my relationship with each has varied. Some have been happy to allow me to conduct a series of interviews but once they were over they no longer wanted to be involved. Busy people have busy lives and research analysis and findings often do not have a high priority for them. As a researcher, learning this by itself has a salutary effect upon the ego and gets one's grand ideas of the importance of one's research enterprise into perspective. In contrast, some teachers have been very interested to know what my life history research reveals about themselves and others. Several of these teachers engaging in life history research as a collaborative venture has led them on a reflective journey of the self, that at times has been painful, but none the less rewarding for that. Some of the teachers have become my friends. Such points signal that there are major ethical issues to be considered in relation to life history research. As Soltis (1990) comments:

> *Ethics is ubiquitous. It permeates all aspects of our lives......General ethical principles are applicable across the board. They may achieve a pungency in certain research settings, but the principles of honesty, justice, and respect for persons, for example, are not unique to qualitative research. However, there may be typical, repeated sets of qualitative research circumstances that give rise to research-specific ethical dilemmas regarding such things as deception, the propriety of intervention, possible harm to participants, contract obligations, informed consent, and even social rights and wrongs. Some of these are more general and no doubt occur across many qualitative research settings. Others may be more likely to arise only in special settings. (pp. 247-248).*

In a similar fashion, Burgess (1989) claims, 'It is difficult for researchers to deny that ethical, moral and political questions do not surround their day to day experience of education and educational research' (p.1). Likewise, Glesne & Peshkin (1992) argue that while ethical dilemmas and considerations defy any easy solution they, 'are inseparable from your everyday interactions with your others and with your data' (p. 109). All this is particularly true for life history research which by its very nature depends on the social relationships developed between the story teller and the research as they explore a life. Given that I have focused on these issues in detail elsewhere (see Sparkes, 1994b) only a few of the ethical dilemmas associated with life history research will be considered here. My intention is to highlight the need for all those choosing to engage in life history research to seriously consider the ethical dimensions to their work with teachers.

RESEARCHER AS THERAPIST?

Often life history research involves prolonged contact with participants and this can lead to various forms of emotional support being offered. For example, during my interviews with Jessica (the lesbian PE teacher) , she shared with me many of the frustrations, tensions, and dilemmas she was experiencing as a new entrant into the teaching profession. In one interview she spoke of her 'misery' and her worries about using the term 'depressed' to describe herself. As often happens, this led to a sharing of stories in which I outlined to her my own family history of depression. We also discussed the conditions that were making her 'depressed' and considered how these might be altered. In terms of our interactions Jessica commented, ' I think by doing this, right now, right here, is almost therapy in a sense. By just talking to somebody. You don't actually need answers, it's just the process isn't it'. Several weeks later I received a card from Jessica that joked about the therapeutic dimensions of our interviews. Jessica is not the only participant to use this term in relation to being involved in life history interviews, and other participants have often used the term 'catharsis' to describe the experience of reflecting and working through moments in their lives.

While I do not see myself as a therapist it would be foolish to deny that this element of our relationship remains. Others have also noted this feature of life history interviews. For example, Measor and Sikes (1992) comment, 'One of the issues that emerged was the way that some of our respondents took advantage of the counselling potential of the interview sessions. There were some limited points of comparison with a Rogerian style of counselling, in that we listened, reflected back, asked questions which encouraged people to reflect on their actions and did not pass judgment' (p. 226). Similarly, Glesne & Peshkin (1992) point out, 'Although researchers do not wittingly assume the role of therapist, they nonetheless fashion an interview process that can be strikingly therapeutic' (p. 123). However, Goodson (1992c) has expressed concern over the therapeutic dimension of life history work as a trading point.

> *This intersection with the psychological or psychoanalytical approach opens up new and, I believe, potentially perilous terrain for collaboration......If the co-partners in a collaboration treat sessions as counselling or therapy sessions this has implications for the research study.......Counselling/therapy in short would push us in one direction, research in another. This distinction must be made clear early in the collaborative pact......In general the ethical and methodological dilemmas I have noted would be best dealt with through clear procedural guidelines' (pp. 246-247).*

Unfortunately, Goodson (1992c) is less clear about the forms these procedural guidelines should take in relation to counselling/therapy and research. Indeed, the issue of emphasising 'procedure' early on in a research process, in which neither of the participants knows where it will take them, seems something of a preemptive measure which might act to constrain the very forms of relationship that life history work depends on to provide insights and understanding. For example, with regard to my emerging relationship with Jessica that has changed significantly over the last three years, would any procedural guidelines drawn up when we were student and lecturer have been of much use? Would they have negated any shift in the relationship later on? As Jessica notes, 'The story keeps on changing'. Finally, given the dynamic interplay that goes on in life history interviews which often focus on issues of the 'self', there is the complex issue of knowing just when 'research' becomes 'therapy'. In many cases such matters are only made evident on reflection after the event. As a consequence, the epistemological gap between research and therapy may be less clearly defined than Goodson would wish it to be once dialogue is under way and people get involved in a story that can explore, and expose, deep aspects of the self and identity.

The previous points also hold true for researchers who can often gain insights into their own self development by listening to the stories of others. That is, the interaction can also serve a therapeutic function for the researcher as well as the subject. Given that life historians cannot remain as distant and detached as some people would like and often seek a close and sympathetic involvement with those they work with, then perhaps Measor and Sikes (1992) raise one of the most important issues for this form of engagement when they comment, 'It does seem that there is a responsibility there, which should be acknowledged - and that is a basic human responsibility to other people. We should not initiate situations that we are not prepared to see through to their potential conclusion' (p. 226).

CAN WE BE FRIENDS?

Often, due to the nature and extended periods of their interactions, life history researchers form close relationships with the participants in their study. As Glesne & Peshkin (1992) point out, 'Researchers often have friendly relationships with their others; in some cases, the relationship is one of friendship. Whether friendship or friendliness is the case, ethical dilemmas can result' (p. 117). For example, Jessica and I are now friends and in many ways my responsibilities as researcher for her become even more intensified. Delamont (1992) reminds us that the choice of pseudonyms for those participating in our research is an important matter. This choice can have symbolic significance for those involved. My own daughter is called Jessica and she was 14 months old when I first began writing part of 'Jessica's story'. By using my daughter's name I was signalling my respect and friendship for a person who, due to oppressive structures was denied a voice to speak openly about herself. On reflection, this choice of name also signalled a growing sense of responsibility I felt for 'Jessica' as part of a caring relationship that was characterised by trust, responsibility and response.

Of course, friendships of any kind bring their own problems and often the closer the relationship, the riskier it is to tell the friend certain stories about oneself. Furthermore, even if friends agree that a story may be published there might be limits that friendship imposes on what can be told. In relation to this Acker et al (1983) point to a usually unarticulated tension between friendships and the goal of research in which the researcher's goal is always to gather information, 'thus the danger always exists of manipulating friendship to that end' (p. 428). In a similar fashion, Stacey (1988) notes.

> *Precisely because ethnographic research depends upon human relationships, engagement, and attachment, it places the research subjects at grave risk of manipulation and betrayal by the ethnographer....The lives, loves, and tragedies that fieldwork informants share with the researcher are ultimately data, grist for the ethnographic mill, a mill that has a truly grinding power (p. 23).*

These tensions and dilemmas are even more pronounced when the friend is in a vulnerable situation, like Jessica, who fears that she would suffer discrimination and ultimately lose her job if colleagues found out that she is a lesbian. There is also a need to care about the other people who become part of Jessica's story, for example, those in her school who she comes out to and seeks support from. Likewise her partner and her friends also need to be protected as the story unfolds. These are vital issues for Measor and Sikes (1992) who comment, 'it is the intimacy which raises some of the sharpest ethical questions in this kind of research. Because the material is intimate, it means that the potential for harm is much greater' (p. 210). They add, 'If we collect information which is otherwise "secret", it does raise questions about the use to which that knowledge is put' (p. 229). Therefore, we need to ask in relation to life history work, what can be learned from others about the personal lives of teachers and to what extent should the personal be made public? These are important questions since they raise the spectre of life historians unwittingly engaging in work that acts as a form of surveillance by providing information on those who have little power in our society to those who have greater power. Such issues become particularly pertinent once the process begins of writing about aspects of a life for public consumption.

WRITING LIVES: THE POLITICS OF REPRESENTATION

Writing about the lives of others is not just a technical or methodological issue since the end product has *moral* consequences for those involved. While such issues apply to writing the lives of all teachers they are particularly acute in relation to researchers writing about people who belong to social categories to which they do not belong. My writing about, and for, Jessica (see Sparkes 1994a, 1994b) crystallises some of these issues. For example, how do I write a life? How do I portray Jessica? How do I write in such a way as to convey the pain, injustices and struggles that Jessica experiences? Indeed, why do I write and what right have I got, as a male heterosexual, to write about her life at all? If I write, what would be the consequences of my writing? What do I hope to achieve through my writing? These and other associated ethical dilemmas come into sharp relief in the creation of a textual product.

Despite my many conversations with Jessica, and despite the fact that she has read, commented on, and agreed with the interpretations I have presented in any work I have produced about her life, tensions still remain. These tensions revolve around the attendant dilemmas of authorship that have been signalled by scholars influenced by postmodernism. After all, it is 'I' who wrote the story, identified the recurrent theme of 'being out and being me' from the interview transcripts, and selected those particular passages that related to this issue in terms of Jessica's use of coping strategies in contexts characterised by varying degrees of homophobia and heterosexism. As Hastrup (1992) comments with regard to ethnographic writing, 'It is *our* choice to encompass their stories in a narrative of a different order. *We* select the quotations and edit the statements' (p. 122). Indeed, Stacey (1988) in her discussion of the exploitation inherent in the ethnographic method argues that while this approach appears to, and often does, place the researcher and the subjects in a collaborative, reciprocal quest for understanding, the research *product* is ultimately that of the researcher - regardless of how modified or influenced it is by the subjects. She notes, 'With very rare exceptions it is the researcher who narrates, who "authors" the ethnography. In the last instance an ethnography is a written document structured primarily by a researcher's purposes, offering a researcher's interpretation, registered in a researcher's voice' (p. 23). Likewise, Atkinson (1992) points out, 'The encounter between ethnographer and Alter, from this perspective, is not a dialogue. The ethnographer's is the dominant voice. The ethnography is determined by the "point of view" of the ethnographer, (p. 40).

These issues worried me. After all, my concern was to create an arena for Jessica's voice and story to be heard by others who would not normally hear her tale. Yet, I was constantly in danger of shaping her voice, and story, in how and what I wrote from my own social positioning, which in its own way was an echo of my privileged voice over hers. As Dewar (1991) comments:

> *The problem arises when we define our strategy against oppression as one that enables us to "give" certain groups a voice. What does it mean to give? What kinds of relations does this imply? What kind of power and privilege is implied in the act of giving? What does it say about how voices are heard and interpreted? (p. 75).*

How are such issues to be addressed? Despite my many discussions with Jessica about the text and her support for my efforts I could not escape the fact that I was responsible for the final version and that, as Gorelick (1991) and Stacey (1988) have argued, this responsibility was unavoidable. In particular, the 'frozen text' I produced raised the key issue of my authority to write about and for an individual who is a member of a group to which I do not belong. Commenting upon this dilemma, Richardson (1990) notes, 'For whom do we speak and to whom do we speak, with what voice, to what end, using what criteria?..........How does our writing reproduce a system of domination, and how does it challenge that system? What right do we have to speak for others? To write their lives?' (p. 27).

For Richardson (1990) proposals to still the sociologist as writer's voice are in danger of rejecting the value of sociological insight and also implies that somehow facts can exist without interpretation. She suggests that there is no one 'right' answer to the problem of speaking for others and we are left having to realise that writing, as an intentional behaviour, is a site of moral responsibility and that, 'We can choose to write so that the voice of those we write about is respected, strong and true' (p. 38).

Richardson goes on to emphasise that while all knowledge is partial, embodied and historically and culturally situated this does not mean that there is no knowledge, or that situated knowledge is bad.

> *Rather than decrying our socio-historical limitations, then, we can use them specifically to ask relevant (useful, empowering, enlightening) questions. Consequently, the most pressing issue, as I see it, is a practical-ethical one: how should we use our skills and privileges........As qualitative researchers, we can more easily write as situated, positioned authors, giving up, if we choose, our* authority *over the people we study, but not the responsibility of* authorship *over our* texts. *(pp.27-28).*

Others have also emphasised that the responsibility of authorship remains with the researcher while Glesne & Peshkin (1992) suggest that if we attempt to write honestly and cogently about those who allow us into their lives, then this is an ethically defendable position. In considering whether people occupying different social positions can research with and write about each other's lives Sears (1992) raises some key questions that do not revolve around one's ability to remain objective but one's capacity to be empathetic. He suggests that the proper questions are, 'Have you immersed yourself in the world of the other? Have you portrayed its richness and complexity? Have you treated your informants/characters with respect and understanding?......conveying with integrity their understandings of their many worlds' (p. 149).

The comments by Sears echo the thoughts of Barone (1992) concerning the involvement of academics in the production of honest, and critical storytelling, that enables both writer and reader to locate the beating, and the aching, of other human hearts within a debilitating and unjust sociopolitical milieu. For Barone, if academics are to be worthy of their privileges then one of their primary responsibilities is to speak for those who cannot speak for themselves so that the reader can achieve *solidarity* with them as fellow human beings. This involves describing how the life-worlds of people who appear as strangers are shaped by particular webs of contingencies. Such honest, responsible, critical and compelling stories, he believes, are openly political in that they have as their ultimate aim the empowerment of the powerless and the transformation of existing social inequalities and injustices.

REFLECTING ON ETHICAL ISSUES IN LIFE HISTORY RESEARCH

The ethical dilemmas I have presented in relation to my own life history research would suggest that various formalised codes of ethical principles are useful in terms of providing a framework for reflection on fieldwork and sensitising the researcher to areas that may be problematic. However, the point I would make is that all these general principles are ultimately enacted, and interpreted, in the dynamics of the research process at a micro level as people interact with each other. At this level one has to live one's ethics in relation to others. This is no easy task as there is no rule book to cover all situations and eventualities.

So where does all of this leave us in terms of ethics? Here, it is worth considering the work of Plummer (1983) who identifies two broad positions in relation to research ethics; the *ethical absolutist* and the *situational relativist*. The former seeks to establish firm principles which should *guide* all social research and feel that these principles should be *encoded* in professional charters that are absolutely necessary to protect both the community and the researcher. In contrast, the situational relativists suggest that the ethical dilemmas of the researcher are not 'special' but co-terminous with everyday life. Therefore, from this stance there can be no absolute guidelines and ethics have to be produced *creatively in the concrete situation at hand*. Plummer argues that there are weaknesses in both positions and suggests a combination of the two 'On balance, I suggest, some broad guidelines should be presented collectively by professional bodies, but these should always allow plenty of room (but not absolute room) for personal ethical choice by the researcher' (p. 141). I would agree, and would further endorse the views of Glesne & Peshkin (1992) who argue:

> *Ethical codes certainly guide research behaviour, but the degree to which research is or is not ethical depends on the researcher's continual communication and interaction with research participants. Researchers alone must not be the arbiters of this critical research issue (p. 125).*

At the end of the day there are no simple solutions to the ethical dilemmas encountered by life history researchers. There is no easy way out, nor should there be if we wish to continue to engage in a dynamic process and produce textual products that have consequences for the lives of others as well as our own.

CLOSING COMMENTS

In drawing this monograph to a close I hope that I have been able to indicate some of the strengths and potentials of the life history approach for understanding teachers, and that you will consider this to be a worthwhile and justifiable approach in and of itself for your future research endeavours. However, it would be foolish to view its analytical power in isolation and there is a need to recognise that life history work can form a range of complementary relationships with other kinds of research, such as critical theory and phenomenology. Indeed, in relation to the former the two can combine to initiate change at both the individual and the societal levels. Likewise, life history research can be used with with more 'experimental' or quantitative approaches. All are taken to be legitimate epistemologies that are able, both individually and in suitable combination, to provide a rich understanding of educational life. This is not to deny the fundamental tensions that exist between some of these approaches. However, I suggest that each has its story to tell. In this sense the research enterprise should not be viewed as monolithic but as multi-faceted. Goodson (1988, p. 80) draws upon the imagery of the mosaic and the jigsaw to locate the place of life histories and suggests that 'By rehabilitating the life history the jigsaw puzzle might finally fall into place, for there is always a better chance if all the pieces are used'. I could not agree more.

REFERENCES

Acker, J, Barry, K. & Esseveld, J. (1983) Objectivity and truth: problems in doing feminist research, Woman's Studies International Forum, 6, pp. 423-435.

Acker, S. (1989) Rethinking teachers' careers. In:S. Acker (Ed) Teacher, Gender and Careers Lewes: Falmer Press.

Acker, S. (1990) Women teachers at work. Paper presented at the Canadian Teachers' Federation, Women in Education Conference, Vancouver, BC, November.

Apple, M. (1979) Ideology and Curriculum London: Routledge & Kegan Paul.

Atkinson, P. (1992) Understanding Ethnographic Texts London: Sage.

Ball, S. (1987) The Micro-Politics of the School London: Methuen.

Ball, S. & Goodson, I. (Eds.) (1985) Teachers' Lives and Careers Lewes: Falmer Press.

Barone, T. (1992) Beyond theory and method: a case of critical storytelling, Theory Into Practice, XXXI (2), pp. 142-146.

Becker, H. (1966) Introduction to The Jack Roller by Clifford Shaw, Chicago: University of Chicago Press. In H. Becker (1971) Sociological Work London: Allen Lane.

Bensimon, E. (1992) Lesbian existence and the challenge to normative constructions of the academy, Journal of Education, 174(3), pp.98-113.

Benyon, J. (1985) Institutional change and career histories in a comprehensive school. In: S.Ball & I. Goodson (Eds) Teachers' Lives and Careers Lewes: Falmer Press.

Bertaux, D. (Ed) (1981) Biography and Society London: Sage.

Burgess, R. (1989) (Ed) The Ethics of Educational Research. Lewes: Falmer Press

Burrell, G. & Hearn, J. (1989) The sexuality of organization. In: J. Hearn, D. Sheppard, P.Tancred-Sheriff & G. Burrell (Eds) The Sexuality of Organization London: Sage.

Burrell, G. & Morgan, G. (1979) Sociological Paradigms and Organizational Analysis London: Heinemann.

Butt, R. (1989) An integrative function for teachers' biographies. In G. Milburn, I. Goodson & R. Clark (Eds) Reinterpreting Curriculum and Research: Images and Arguments Lewes: Falmer Press.

Butt, R. & Raymond, D. (1987) Arguments for using qualitative approaches in understanding teacher thinking: the case for biography, Journal of Curriculum Theorizing, 7, pp. 62-94.

Connell, R. (1985) Teachers' Work London: George Allen & Unwin.

Cunnison, S. (1985) Making It In a Man's World: Women Teachers in a Senior High School. University of Hull, Department of Sociology and Anthropology, Occasional Paper No 1.

Corradi, C. (1991) Text, context and individual meaning: rethinking life stories in a hermeneutic framework, Discourse and Society, 2, pp. 105-118.

Department of Education and Science (1982) The secondary school staffing survey, Statistical Bulletin, 5/82, March, London: HMSO.

Delamont, S. (1992) Fieldwork in Educational Settings: Methods, Pitfalls & Perspectives Lewes: Falmer Press.

De Lyon, H. & Migniuolo, F. (Eds.), (1989) Women Teachers: Issues and Experiences Milton Keynes: Open University Press.

Dewar, A. (1991) Feminist pedagogy in physical education: promises, possibilities and pitfalls, Journal of Physical Education, Recreation and Dance, 62, pp. 68-71.

Dewar, A. (1993) Would all the generic women in sport please stand up? Challenges facing feminist sport sociology, Quest, 45, pp. 211-229.

Elbaz, F. (1990) Knowledge and discourse: the evolution of research on teacher thinking. In Day, C., Pope, M., & Denicolo, P. (Eds) Insight into Teachers' Thinking and Practice Lewes: Falmer Press.

Evans, J. & Williams, T. (1989) Moving up and getting out: the classed and gendered career opportunities of physical education. In T. Templin & P. Schempp (Eds) Socialization into Physical Education: Learning to Teach. Indianapolis: Benchmark Press.

Faraday, A. & Plummer, K. (1979) Doing life histories, Sociological Review, 27, pp. 773-98.

Giddens, A. (1979) Central Problems in Social Theory Berkeley, CA: University of California Press.

Giddens, A. (1984) The Constitution of Society Cambridge: Cambridge University Press.

Giroux, H. (1983) Theory and Resistance in Education London: Heinemann

Glesne, C. & Peshkin, A. (1992) Becoming Qualitative Researchers: An Introduction London: Longman.

Goodson, I. (1981) Life histories and the study of schooling, Interchange, 11, pp. 62-76.

Goodson, I. (1983) The use of life histories in the study of schooling. In: M. Hammersley (Ed.), Ethnography and Schooling . Driffield: Nafferton.

Goodson, I. (1984) Beyond the subject monolith: subject traditions and subcultures. In: P.Harling (Ed) New Directions in Educational Leadership Lewes: Falmer Press.

Goodson, I. (1988) The Making of Curriculum: Collected Essays Lewes: Falmer Press.

Goodson, I. (1991a) Sponsoring the teacher's voice: teachers' lives and teacher development, Cambridge Journal of Education, 21, pp. 35-45.

Goodson, I. (1991b) Teachers' lives and educational research. In I. Goodson & R. Walker (Eds) Biography, Identity & Schooling: Episodes in Educational Research Lewes: Falmer Press.

Goodson, I. (Ed.) (1992a) Studying Teachers' Lives London: Routledge.

Goodson, I. (1992b) Studying teachers' lives: an emergent field of inquiry. In I. Goodson (Ed) Studying Teachers' Lives London: Routledge.

Goodson, I. (1992c) Studying teachers' lives: problems and possibilities. In I. Goodson (Ed) Studying Teachers' Lives . London: Routledge.

Goodson, I. & Walker, R. (1991) Biography, Identity and Schooling: Episodes in Educational Research Lewes: Falmer Press.

Gorelick, S. (1991) Contradictions of feminist methodology, Gender & Society, 5, pp. 459-477.

Griffin, P. (1991) Identity management strategies among lesbian and gay educators, International Journal of Qualitative Studies in Education, 4, pp. 189-202.

Griffin, P. (1992a) Lesbian and gay educators: opening the classroom closet, Empathy, 3, pp. 25-28.

Griffin, P. (1992b) Changing the game: homophobia, sexism, and lesbians in sport,

Quest, 44, pp. 251-265.

Griffin, P. & Genasci, J. (1990) Addressing homophobia in physical education: Responsibilities for teachers. In M. Messner & D. Sabo (Eds) Sport, Men and the Gender Order: Critical Feminist Perspectives Champaign, IL: Human Kinetics Press.

Hall, M. (1989) Private experiences in the public domain: lesbians in organizations. In: J.Hearn, D. Sheppard, P. Tancred-Sheriff & G. Burrell (Eds) The Sexuality of Organization London: Sage.

Harding, S. (1991) Whose Science? Whose Knowledge? Milton Keynes: Open University Press.

Hastrup, K. (1992) Writing ethnography: state of the art. In J. Okely & H. Callaway (Eds) Anthropology & Autobiography London: Routledge.

Hearn, J. (1987) The Gender of Oppression, Brighton: Harvester Wheatsheaf.

Hoyle, E. (1986) Curriculum development in physical education 1966-1985. In <u>Trends and Developments in Physical Education</u>. Proceedings of the VIIIth Commonwealth and International Conference on Sport, Physical Education, Dance, Recreation and Health. London: E. & F.N. Spon.

Khayatt, M. (1992) <u>Lesbian Teachers: An Invisible Presence</u> State University: New York Press.

Kitzinger, C. (1987) <u>The Social Construction of Lesbianism</u> London: Sage.

Langness, L. & Frank G. (1981) <u>Lives: An Anthropological Approach to Biography</u> Novato, CA: Chandler & Sharp Publishers Inc.

Lenskyj, H. (1991) Combating homophobia in sport and physical education, <u>Sociology of Sport Journal</u>, 8, pp. 61-69.

Mangan, J. (1981) <u>Athleticism in the Victorian and Edwardian Public School</u>. Lewes: Falmer Press.

Mangan, J. & Park, R. (1987) <u>From 'Fair Sex' to Feminism</u> London: Frank Cass.

Marcus, J. (1984) Invisible mending. In: C. Ascher, L. De Salvo & S. Ruddick (Eds) <u>Between Women</u> Boston: Beacon Press.

Marsick, V. (1989) <u>Learning to be: Life history and professionalism</u>. Paper presented at the annual conference of the American Educational Research Association, San Francisco, April.

Measor, L. & Sikes, P. (1992) Visiting lives: ethics and methodology in life history. In I.Goodson (Ed) <u>Studying Teachers' Lives</u> Lewes: Falmer Press.

Munro, P. (1991) <u>Multiple "I's": Dilemmas of Life History Research</u>. Paper presented at the annual American Educational Research Association Conference, Chicago, IL, April.

Nias, J. (1989) <u>Primary Teachers Talking</u> London: Routledge.

Olsen, M. (1987) A study of gay and lesbian teachers, <u>Journal of Homosexuality</u>, 13, pp. 73-81

Plummer, K. (1983) <u>Documents of Life</u> London: Unwin Hyman.

Plummer, K. (1990) Herbert Blumer and the life history tradition, <u>Symbolic Interaction</u>, 13, pp. 125-144.

Pollard, A. (1982) A model of classroom coping strategies, <u>British Journal of Sociology of Education</u>, 3, pp. 19-37.

Richardson, L. (1990) <u>Writing Strategies: Reaching Diverse Audiences</u> London: Sage.

Runyan, W. (1982) <u>Life Histories and Psychobiography</u> Oxford University Press.

Schempp, P., Sparkes, A. & Templin, T. (1993) The micropolitics of teacher induction. American Educational Research Journal, 30 (3), pp. 447-472.

Shilling, C. (1991) Social space, gender inequalities and educational differentiation, British Journal of Sociology of Education, 12, pp. 23-44.

Sears, J. (1992) Researching the other/searching for self: qualitative research on [homo]sexuality in education, Theory Into Practice, XXXI (2), pp. 147-156.

Sikes, P., Measor, L., & Woods, P. (1985) Teachers' Careers: Crises and Continuities Lewes: Falmer Press.

Smith, J. (1989) The Nature of Social and Educational Inquiry: Empiricism Versus Interpretation Norwood, NJ: Albex Publishing Corporation.

Smith, J. (1993) After the Demise of Empiricism: The Problem of Judging Social and Educational Inquiry Norwood, NJ: Albex Publishing Corporation.

Soltis, J. (1990) The ethics of qualitative research. In E. Eisner & A. Peshkin (Eds) Qualitative Inquiry in Education: The Continuing Debate. London: Teachers College Press.

Sparkes, A. (1990a) The changing nature of teachers' work: reflecting on governor power in different historical periods, Physical Education Review, 13 (1), pp. 39-47.

Sparkes, A. (1990b) The emerging relationship between physical education teachers and school governors: a sociological analysis, Physical Education Review, 13 (2), pp. 128-137.

Sparkes, A. (1991) The culture of teaching, critical reflection and change: possibilities and problems, Educational Management and Administration, 19, pp. 4-19.

Sparkes, A. (1992a) The paradigms debate: an extended review and a celebration of difference. In: A. Sparkes (Ed) Research in Physical Education and Sport: Exploring Alternative Visions. Lewes: Falmer Press.

Sparkes, A. (1992b) The changing nature of teachers' work: school governors and curriculum control in physical education. In N. Armstrong (Ed) New Directions in Physical Education (Volume 2): Towards a National Curriculum Champaign, IL: Human Kinetics Press.

Sparkes, A. (1994 a) Self, silence and invisibility as a beginning teacher: a life history of lesbian experience, British Journal of Sociology of Education 15(1), pp.93-118

Sparkes, A. (1994 b) Life histories and the issue of voice: reflections on an emerging relationship, International Journal of Qualitative Studies in Education, 7(2), pp.165-183.

Sparkes, A, & Bloomer, M. (1993) Teacher cultures and school-based management: towards a collaborative reconstruction. In: J. Smyth (Ed) <u>A Socially Critical View of the Self-Managing School</u> Lewes: Falmer Press.

Sparkes A. & Templin, T. (1992) Life histories and physical education teachers: exploring the meanings of marginality. In A Sparkes (Ed) <u>Research in Physical Education and Sport: Exploring Alternative Visions</u> London: Falmer Press.

Sparkes, A., Templin, T., & Schempp, P. (1990) The problematic nature of a career in a marginal subject: some implications for teacher education programmes, <u>Journal of Education for Teaching</u>, 16, pp. 3-28.

Sparkes, A. & Tiihonen, A. (1992) Silent voices in a marginal world: exploring the emancipatory potential of life histories. <u>Proceedings of the 1st ISPHES conference on sport and cultural minorities</u> . Helsinki: Finnish Society for Research in Sport and Physical Education.

Spencer, D. (1986) <u>Contemporary Women Teachers: Balancing School and Home</u> London: Longman.

Squirrell, G. (1989a) In passing.......teachers and sexual orientation. In S. Acker (Ed) <u>Teachers, Gender & Careers</u> Lewes: Falmer Press.

Squirrell, G. (1989b) Teachers and issues of sexual orientation, <u>Gender and Education, 1</u>, pp. 17-34.

Stacey, J. (1988) Can there be a feminist ethnography?, <u>Women's Studies International Forum</u> 11, pp. 21-27.

Templin, T., Sparkes, A., & Schempp, P. (1991) The professional life cycle of a retired physical education teacher: a tale of bitter disengagement, <u>Physical Education Review</u>, 14, pp. 143-156.

Thomas, W. & Znaniecki, F. (1958) <u>The Polish Peasant in Europe and America</u> New York: Dover Publications (original editions published 1918-1920).

Walby, S. (1989) Theorising patriarchy, <u>Sociology,</u> 23, pp. 213-234.

Watson, L & Watson-Franke, M. (1985) <u>Interpreting Life Histories: An Anthropological Inquiry</u> Rutgers University Press: New Brunswick, NJ.

Wolcott, H. (1990) Ethnographic research in education. In: R. Jaeger (Ed) <u>Complementary Methods for Research in Education</u> Washington DC: American Educational Research Association.

Woods, P. (1984) Teacher, self and curriculum. In Goodson, I & Ball, S. (Eds) <u>Defining the Curriculum: Histories and Ethnographies</u> Lewes: Falmer Press.

Woods, P. (1985) Conversations with teachers: some aspects of the life history method. <u>British Educational Research Journal,</u> 11, pp. 13-25.

Woods, P. (1987) Life history and teacher knowledge. In: J. Smyth (Ed) <u>Educating Teachers: Changing the Nature of Pedagogical Knowledge</u> London: Falmer Press.

Woods, S. (1992) Describing the experience of lesbian physical educators: a phenomenological study. In: A. Sparkes (Ed) <u>Research In Physical Education and Sport: Exploring Alternative Visions</u> Lewes: Falmer Press.

ANNOTATED BIBLIOGRAPHY

Acker, S. (Ed) <u>Teachers, Gender & Careers</u> Lewes: Falmer Press

Essential reading for understanding the gender divisions within teaching and how they have historically been structured. Gender is placed at the centre of the debate and discussion about teachers' lives and careers. Various chapters focus upon key theoretical and conceptual issues along with reports of empirical research of both a qualitative and quantitative kind, as well as reflections on personal experience. The book develops an appreciation of both common features and diversity in teachers' experiences and perspectives, as influenced not only by biography and personal characteristics, but also by cultures and educational institutions, labour market conditions for teachers, historical and contemporary educational policy, gender divisions and other social divisions within the wider society. Provides a powerful framework for reconceptualising teachers' careers.

Ball, S. & Goodson, I. (Eds) (1985) <u>Teachers' Lives and Careers</u> Lewes: Falmer Press.

This excellent volume explores the contemporary situation of teachers' careers and teachers' lives in the context of falling rolls, educational cuts and government demands for fundamental change in educational processes. Each chapter provides empirical data that draws upon qualitative observations of life history interviews to reflect the words, experiences and problems facing teachers in schools. Very good for showing how individual lives are shaped by wider social structures.

Burgesss, R. (Ed) (1982) <u>Field Research: A Sourcebook and Field Manual</u> London: George Allen & Unwin.

A very good reader for all those wishing to embark on interpretive forms of enquiry. There is a specific section on historical sources and field research. The section on conversations in field research is also very relevant to life history work.

Burgess, R. (1985) <u>In the Field: An Introduction to Field Research.</u> London: George Allen & Unwin.

Essential reading for those who wish to undertake field research. Contains three chapters that focus on methods of field research, one of which is specifically about the use of personal documents.

Butt, R. (1989) 'An integrative function for teachers' biographies'. In: G.Milburn, I. Goodson & R. Clark (Eds) Re-Interpreting Curriculum Research: Images and Arguments (pp. 146-159) Lewes: Falmer Press.

Focuses on the personal and biographical aspects of teachers' knowledge. Describes and presents a reflective analysis of a graduate-education course that emphasises autobiographical accounts to reveal the personal and experiential nature of teaching. Indicates that this type of study is particularly conducive to research and professional development.

Denzin, N. (1989) Interpretive Biography. London: Sage

A provocative, thoughtful and stimulating book that needs to be read by all life historians. Denzin defines the autobiographical method as the studied use and collection of life documents, or documents of life, which describe turning-point moments in individuals' lives. These documents are taken to include autobiographies, biographies, diaries, letters, obituaries, life histories, life stories, personal experience stories, oral histories, and personal histories. His book provides an overview and critical interpretation of the method and its use in the human discipline. However, this is not a 'how to do it' book, it does not lay out procedures that a researcher might follow when attempting to do a life history. Rather, Denzin focuses upon how biographical texts are written and read. In doing so he highlights that there are many biographical methods, and many ways of writing about a life. Each form presenting different textual problems and leaves the reader with different messages and understandings. In essence, Denzin provides an epistemological critique that has biography as its focus.

Goodson, I. (1983) 'The use of life histories in the study of teaching'. In: M.Hammersley (Ed) The Ethnography of Schooling Driffield: Nafferton Books.

Provides a good overview of the history of life histories and outlines the possibilities and problems of rehabilitating this approach for the study of teachers and teaching.

Goodson, I. (1988) The Making of Curriculum: Collected Essays Lewes: Falmer Press.

Contains several chapters on methodology that outline the potential of life history and curriculum history as forms of research for understanding teachers and schooling.

Goodson, I. (1992) 'Sponsoring the teacher's voice: Teachers' lives and teacher development'. In: A. Hargreaves & M. Fullan (Eds) <u>Understanding Teacher Development</u> (pp. 110-121) London: Cassell.

Makes a very strong case for the study of teachers' lives as central to the study of curriculum and schooling. Emphasises that to understand teacher development and curriculum development, and to tailor it accordingly, we need to know a great deal more about teachers' priorities and more about teachers' lives. The case is made for broadening our data base for studying teaching and listening to the voices of teachers.

In terms of collaborative research between teachers and researchers, Goodson argues that classroom practice is an unpromising entry point since it focuses upon the area of maximum vulnerability for the teacher. Goodson instead suggests that we begin by examining the teacher's work in the context of the teacher's life, as a rich source of dialogue and data. It is claimed that issues of class, gender, lifestyle and life cycle are all formative influences upon teachers and their teaching, and that, these influences need to be acknowledged and be given priority in teacher development work.

Goodson, I. (Ed) (1992) <u>Studying Teachers' Lives</u> London: Routledge.

Provides valuable insights into the range of perspectives available within life history research to make sense of and analyse the lives and work of teachers. Most importantly, each chapter moves beyond 'stories of action' to locate these lives in their wider socio-historical and political contexts to highlight how the impact of new initiatives to restructure and reform schools often run counter to the everyday realities of teachers' lives and the priorities grounded therein. Chapters also discuss key methodological concepts and ethical issues associated with life history research.

Goodson, I. & Walker, R. (1991) <u>Biography, Identity & Schooling: Episodes in Educational Research</u> Lewes: Falmer Press

Contains a series of key essays by both authors over the last twenty years. The common theme between chapters is a concern for biography and history that leads the authors to embark upon a reflective journey of their own in such a way as to display the explanatory power of life history research.

Herr, K. & Anderson, G. (1993) 'Oral history for student empowerment: capturing students' inner voices', <u>International Journal of Qualitative Studies in Education</u>, 6 (3), pp. 185-196.

Through the close analysis of the oral history of Victor, a Hispanic student in an affluent Anglo institution, the authors provide an example of how oral history methods can capture student voices and uncover the silencing that often takes place in well-intentioned educational institutions, and demonstrates how some of the multiple voices that exist within students and school communities are legitimated, while others are not. Drawing on Mikhail Bakhtin's theory of inner voice, the analysis illustrates the potential of oral history methods for probing the multiple voices and lived experiences of students. It suggests how these voices help to reveal how students construct their identities in educational institutions.

Huberman, M. (1992) 'Teacher development and instructional mastery'. In: A. Hargreaves & M. Fullan (Eds) <u>Understanding Teacher Development</u> (pp. 122-142) London: Cassell.

Based on a major study of 160 secondary teachers, Huberman examines the effect of teacher life cycle on teachers' approaches to instruction. He indicates how life cycle concerns are deeply implicated in teachers' approaches to instruction and illustrates this by focusing upon a group of mid-career teachers that are described as 'positive focuser's. Huberman concludes by advocating a 'craft model' for career development and makes suggestions for in-service training based in relation to life cycle concerns.

Plummer, K. (1983) <u>Documents of Life</u> London: Unwin Hyman.

An <u>essential</u> read for anyone contemplating engaging in life history research. Plummer is concerned with the use in social science research of life histories and other types of personal documents which give a first hand account of social experience from the participant's point of view. These materials are taken to be invaluable in providing evidence about the subjective point of view of the social actor, and are seen to be congruent with a theoretical approach in terms of action theory or an action frame of reference. Each chapter provides valuable insights into the conceptual basis of this kind of research along with the practical and ethical dilemmas that researchers are likely to encounter.

Raymond, D., Butt, R. & Townsend, D. (1992)'Contexts for teacher development: insights from teacher stories'. In: A. Hargreaves & M. Fullan (Eds) <u>Understanding Teacher Development</u> (pp. 143-161) London: Cassell.

Emphasises the importance of teachers' lives and teacher biographies and spell out their practical implications for understanding what underpins a teacher's practice, and the process of development that may be necessary to bring about changes in such practice. Provides three rich case studies to illustrate how teaching is profoundly influenced by such things as ethnic background, social class origins, experience of working in other cultures, gender influences, and range and type of previous teaching experiences. Advocates 'collaborative autobiography' as a means to give teachers greater understanding of their own and their colleagues' teaching and how it came to be that way. This approach is also advocated for bringing about change and professional development.

Runyan, W. (1982) <u>Life Histories and Psychobiography: Explorations in Theory and Method</u> Oxford: Oxford University Press.

Examines a number of basic methodological and conceptual problems encountered in the study of life histories in the field of psychobiography. It explores the problems in the description and explanation of individual lives, conceptualisation of the life course, and the critical examination of case study, ideographic, and psychobiographical methods. Theoretical points are vividly illustrated with examples from the lives of, among others, Vincent Van Gogh, Emily Dickinson, Shakespeare, Malcolm X, Virginia Woolf, and several of Freud's classic case studies.

Schempp, P., Sparkes, A. & Templin, T. (1993) 'The micropolitics of teacher induction', <u>American Educational Research Journal</u>. 30 (3), pp. 447-472.

Focuses upon the political events that characterise the start of a teaching career. An interpretive framework is used to access the perceptions and meanings teachers give to experiences encountered in their first years on the job. A life history approach is used to allow three teachers to tell their stories of professional induction. The analysis reveals that teachers' thoughts and actions are influenced and sustained in three streams of consciousness: biography, roles demands, and the school culture. Biography includes experiences drawn upon by teachers in making their way in schools. Role demands pressed upon teachers at two levels: classroom and institutional. Finally, the norms and expectations of the school culture influenced the teachers professional perspectives and standards of practice. Of particular interest for the researchers were the teachers' perceptions of power relationships in schools and the strategies used for appropriating the power and status necessary to become accepted and functioning teachers.

Sikes, P., Measor, L. & Woods, P. (1985) <u>Teacher Careers: Crises and Continuities</u> Lewes: Falmer Press.

A key text which uses the life history approach to develop a model of the life-cycle of the teacher, and shows how 'critical incidents' affect passage through it. It explores how teachers view coping with problems and constraints, and how they adapt to the teacher role. It examines institutional contexts for their effect on teacher careers, and explores other factors (such as teaching subject, pupils, and personal life) that seemed to the teachers concerned to have a bearing on the nature and direction of those careers. Concentrates very much on teachers' own subjective perceptions, over the whole range of the teacher's life, and links these into wider structural events.

Smith, L., Kleine, P., Prunty, J & Dwyer, D. (1986) <u>Educational Innovators: Then and Now</u> Lewes: Falmer Press.

Focuses on belief systems, personalities and life histories of critical participants as part of a 15-year follow up study of a major innovation. Shows clearly the inherent weaknesses of attempts to understand educational change that omit the individual person in the innovative process.

Sparkes, A. (1994) 'Self, silence and invisibility as a beginning teacher: a life history analysis of lesbian experience', <u>British Journal of Sociology of Education</u>, 15 (1), pp. 93-118.

This paper draws upon data from an on-going series of life history interviews with a young lesbian PE teacher, called Jessica (a pseudonym), who has recently started her career in a secondary school. Various moments from her life as told and written are provided in order to present a view of schooling from a particular standpoint that, for the most part, has been repressed. Therefore, how Jessica experiences homophobia and heterosexism in educational institutions, how she relates these experiences to other moments in her life, and the identity management strategies she adopts to cope with specific situations, provide important insights into a reality that is oppositional to the taken-for-granted reality of the dominant and privileged sexual class in schools, that is, heterosexuals. These insights illustrate how Jessica is systematically denied an essential freedom that is systematically granted to heterosexual teachers in a way that legitimises a distinction between her private and public lives that is partial, distorting and perverse. It is concluded that taking action against homophobia and heterosexism is the responsibility of all educators regardless of their sexual identity. This paper, by integrating interactionist concerns with notions of a critical social science, attempts to locate the life of the individual in a wider social context with a view to creating social change.

Sparkes, A. (1994) 'Life histories and the issue of voice: reflections on an emerging relationship', <u>International Journal of Qualitative studies in Education</u>, 7 (2), pp.165-183.

As part of the on-going revival of interest in life history research this paper problematises the issue of voice in this form of enquiry. It does so by acknowledging the differences between life stories and life histories while simultaneously emphasising their essential linkage within a developmental process that is grounded in the relationships that can emerge between researcher and subject. Issues of voice, and the potential for individual and social change in the transition from life story to life history are highlighted by considering an emerging relationship between a white, lesbian, physical educator and a white, male, heterosexual researcher in terms of biographical positioning, sharing stories and building trust, collaboration, researcher as therapist, friendship, and the postmodern dilemmas of representation and authorship. It is suggested that the transition from life story to life history should not be viewed as a linear trouble-free process but one that can have unpredictable consequences for those involved. Throughout the analysis a range of ethical and methodological dilemmas are signalled that need careful consideration by life historians.

Sparkes, A. & Bloomer, M. (1993) 'Teaching cultures and school-based management: towards a collaborative reconstruction'. In J. Smyth (Ed) <u>A Socially Critical View of the *Self-Managing School*</u> Lewes: Falmer Press.

Draws upon moments from the life history of one physical educator and her relationship with school governors in two different historical periods to show the dramatic shift in control that is occurring over teachers' work. By contextualising the life of this one teacher, the authors illustrate the movement from licensed autonomy to regulated autonomy under the symbolic canopy of local management of schools, and pose questions about the deprofessionalisation of teachers that is currently under way. It is suggested that teachers, through recognising the specialist nature of their work, can challenge the new orthodoxies and demonstrate to the public the qualitative effects of the changes associated with the contrived collegiality of the new managerialism in education and other forms of entrepreneurship.

Sparkes, A. & Templin, T. (1992) 'Life histories and physical education teachers'. In A. Sparkes (Ed) <u>Research in Physical Education and Sport: Exploring Alternative Visions</u> (pp. 118-145) Lewes: Falmer Press.

Draws upon data from an on-going study of the lives and careers of physical education teachers to focus upon the dialectical relationship between subjective and objective careers and how these operate to shape the the views and prospects of those who teach a low status subject in schools. As part of this process the personal views of PE teachers from different generations, regarding their marginality and positioning of their subject relative to others, are located in a historical landscape to reveal how their personal troubles are linked to broader social issues. The chapter concludes by considering the potential for life histories to empower teachers and initiate change by providing a forum for their voices in the research process.

Sparkes, A., Templin, T. & Schempp, P. (1990) 'The problematic nature of a career in a marginal subject: some implications for teacher education programmes'. <u>Journal of Education for Teaching</u>, 16 (1), pp. 3-28.

In Western cultures subjects defined as practical have had consistent difficulty in gaining acceptance within the curriculum. These subjects have been marginalised and accorded low status, which has influenced their positioning in relation to other subjects in terms of the allocation of power, resources and funding in schools. For those who choose to teach such subjects the construction of a career is highly problematic. Utilising a life history approach this paper focuses upon the experiences and concerns of a range of physical education (PE) teachers at different stages of their careers and the manner in which they respond to perceptions of marginality. A strong classroom orientation is seen to be held on entry into teaching, which informs the dominant response of strategic compliance that reduces the capacity of these teachers to challenge and transform the structures that constrain them. The role of initial teacher education programmes in reproducing this process is discussed and it is suggested that they provide a partial and misleading picture of the realities of school life for those destined to teach this subject. It is argued that these programmes need to develop a critical enquiry perspective, and make explicit the micropolitical nature of a career in a marginal subject, so that physical education teachers may be adequately resourced with a knowledge base that stimulates their awareness of the ways in which power and interests operate in the educational system.

Templin, T., Sparkes, A. & Schempp, P. (1991) 'The professional life cycle of a retired physical education teacher: a tale of bitter disengagement'. <u>Physical Education Review,</u> 14 (2), pp. 143-156.

Explores the life history of a retired PE teacher and locates his growing disillusionment to changes in the wider culture. By revealing how these changes, which are beyond his control, shape his life in school we are able to gain glimpses of the dynamic interplay between social structure and agency. Simultaneously, the outcomes of this interplay in terms of this teacher's bitter disengagement from the profession begin to question standard models of what it is to have a career in teaching.

Woods, P. (1984) 'Teacher, self and curriculum'. In: I. Goodson & S. Ball (Eds) <u>Defining the Curriculum: Histories and Ethnographies</u> (pp. 239-261). Lewes: Falmer Press

Provides life history material that concentrates on the career of one Art teacher, called Tom, to isolate and examine some of the strategies, trade-offs, gains and losses, that produce and constrain this teacher's view of, and involvement in, his subject. The main focus of the chapter is on the teacher's self, the expression, investment and realisation of the person in school and classroom work.

Woods, P. (1987) 'Life histories and teacher knowledge'. In: J. Smyth (Ed) <u>Educating Teachers: Changing the Nature of Pedagogical Knowledge</u> (pp. 121-135). Lewes: Falmer Press

Provides a powerful rationale for life history research as a means of constructing meaningful, relevant and living teacher knowledge. Also emphasises how life histories can inform our thinking about one's ability to explore how notions of the self engage with wider social structures.

 **READER**

American Educational Research Journal, 1993, Vol. 30, No. 3, PP. 447-472

The Micropolitics of Teacher Induction

Paul G. Schempp *University of Georgia*, Andrew C. Sparkes *University of Exeter*
Thomas J. Templin *Purdue University*

PAUL G. SCHEMPP is the Director of the Curriculum and Instruction Research Laboratory in the Physical Education Building at the University of Georgia, Athens, GA 30602. His specialization is teacher socialization.

ANDREW C. SPARKES is a Senior Lecturer in the School of Education at Exeter University, Exeter, Devon, EXI 2LU, England. His specializations are educational innovation, micropolitics of school life, and teachers' lives and careers.

THOMAS J. TEMPLIN is a Professor in the Department of Health, Kinesiology, and Leisure Studies at Purdue University, West La Fayette, IN 47907 His specialization is teacher socialization.

This study, investigated the political events characterizing the start of a teaching career. An interpretative framework was used to access the perceptions and meanings teachers gave to experiences encountered in their first years on the job. Life history methodology permitted three teachers to tell their stories of professional induction. Data analysis revealed that the teachers' thoughts and actions were influenced and sustained in three streams of consciousness: biography), role demands, and the school culture. Biography included experiences drawn upon by teachers in making their way in schools. Role demands pressed upon the teachers at two levels: classroom and institutional. Finally, the norms and expectations of school culture influenced the teachers' professional perspectives and standards of practice. Of particular interest to the researchers were the teachers' perceptions of the power relationships in schools and the strategies used for appropriating the power and status necessary to become accepted and functioning school teachers.

The first years in any occupation represent an important formative period.

It is no different for teachers. During this time newcomers must prove their mettle in the work place, and if they execute their duties within the conventions of accepted practice while displaying a proper demeanour, they are usually accorded full-member status.

Successful initiates adopt ways of thinking and acting that place them in harmony with the existing occupational culture. The inductee joins an established group and in so doing changes the complexion and delicate social balance of the group. Acceptance of the inductee depends on his or her being viewed as a positive addition.

Novice teachers often find their beliefs vigorously challenged as they attempt to meet the demands and expectations pressed upon them by schools (Veeneman, 1984). The dialectic process of induction reshapes the actions and beliefs of both the individual and institution (Schempp & Graber, 1992). New members change as they affiliate with an institution, and the organization changes as new members usher in fresh ideas and unique ways of acting. Dialectic tension emerge as practices, perspectives, and convictions are tested by the potent demands of life in school. Neither individual or institution completely transform, however, because induction is a process of synthesis and adaptation for both.

The dialectics of induction instigate a shift in the social relations of the group. Popkewitz (1987) noted that "The notion of power relates not to ownership but to the understanding of changing social relations and innumerable vantage-points from which power is exercised"(p. 5). Underpinning, directing, and defining the shifting social relationships found in the micropolitics of induction is social power. In shaping their roles in schools, beginning teachers struggle both to understand and exercise power within the school culture. As new members function in the work-site culture, value is given to their opinions and services as their status in the school becomes defined. The greater the status achieved by a member, the greater the influence in shaping the thoughts and actions of the group. For inductees, social power is a necessary prerequisite for both their daily functioning and their long-term acceptance in the school.

The methods of power distribution among its members represent the political economy of a group. For example, authoritarian groups use a political economy that centralizes power into the hands of only a few, or perhaps even just one member. Democratic groups employ methods that distribute power more equitably among their members. New members must learn and use the group's political economy to gain member status and influence within the group. Likewise, the induction of new members signals a shift in power within the group as new members gain and exercise influence over the group. Because of its potential for dramatic change, the induction of new members represents an important item on the political agenda of schools.

Our purpose in conducting this study was to describe and reconstruct the thoughts and actions of three beginning teachers as they negotiated their occupational induction. We attempted to uncover what Hoyle (1982) described as the micropolitical world of occupational life. In other words, this study of teacher induction sought out those "strategies by which individuals and groups in organizational contexts seek to use their resources of power and influences to further their interests" (p. 88). Particular attention was given to both the social pressures and tensions that plied upon these teachers and the teachers' efforts to conform or confront the expectations they met in schools.

Analytic Perspective

The analytic perspective guiding data collection and analysis followed the interpretive/hermeneutic tradition. An interpretive analysis provides a window for viewing the teachers' renditions of their in-school experiences. Knowledge gained from such an analysis can: (a) reveal the contextual social rules and assumptions that underlie teachers' actions, (b) identify the social norms and expectations that bound the range of acceptable actions, and (c) reveal how actions are, or will be, perceived by others in the school (Ewert, 1991).

Mindful of Habermas's (1981) critique, two limitations to interpretive science were noted. First, the interpretive approach depends heavily on the subjective understanding of the individuals of the study. In this regard the perception of reality contained in this article is limited, for we analyzed only the teachers' version of reality. Second, conflicts between the teachers and those in their teaching environment can only be viewed as points of disagreement or misunderstandings. Larger structural issues are ignored because the interpretive view sees reality from one perspective only (the teachers'). Conflicts between teachers and others are not seen as differences in rationality (i.e., ways of knowing or believing). The interpretive framework, therefore, fixes teachers in schools as they exist. It lacks transformative power because it cannot suggest alternative forms of rationality. Given its limitations, the perspective still appeared appropriate for this study because it allowed us to understand, from the teacher's point of view, the micropolitics of occupational induction.

Because this study represents an analysis of micropolitics, attention focused on the induetees' interpretations of-the power relations in schools. Foucault (1970) suggested that there are fundamental codes of culture that govern a society's discourse, modes of interaction, and values. These cultural codes form *a regime of truth*. They inform members as to what can be said and what must be left unsaid, which practices are acceptable and which are unacceptable, and the criteria for distinguishing between truth and error. It is the micropolitics of a group that incubates the establishment and operation of regimes of truth.

Searching for the cultural codes in the discourse and interpretations of induction seems particularly well-suited to this study. As Popkewitz (1987) noted:

> *The problem of socialization lies with how the social production of meaning takes place. As people participate in the world, they continually react to the structures of language and practice, adopting a stance to social affairs that can glorify existing institutions or seek alternatives or oppositional structure. (p. 6)*

This study follows and was inspired by a long line of research in teacher socialization (Zeichner & Gore, 1990). Lacey's (1977) classic work on the social strategies of teachers offered a helpful framework for this study as did the recent expansion of Lacey's work by Zeichner, Tabachnick, and Densmore (1987). However, in keeping with our commitment to allow the teachers to speak for themselves, and following the recommendations of Wolcott (1990) and those who use life-history methodology (Goodson, 1992; Marsick, 1989), we decided to allow the teachers' words to tell this story rather than screening their unique histories through a priori categories. Mindful of this literature, however, we found comparing the present findings with previous work useful for gaining confidence in our conclusions and insight into teachers lives.

Public school teaching takes place in a complex social situation, with each class, school and community offering a distinct constellation of social conditions. Generalizable principles applicable to all teachers are simply not possible. Similar experiences may, however, beget similar interpretations and in turn lead teachers to adopt similar social strategies as they accept, negotiate, change, and adapt to school life. When the shared meanings teachers give to their work are set against the backdrop of a teacher's personal experience in school, a greater understanding of the teaching act is gained. And from this understanding can come the insight necessary for conscious and constructive change in the way teachers are inducted into schools.

Method

Life-history was the chosen research method for this study. Life-history provides an avenue for accessing data necessary for reconstructing the meanings and interpretations teachers give their experiences. Life-history, as Marsick (1989) noted, attends to the concerns of the interpretive tradition, for it reveals the perspectives of people in the social situation of interest. Inspired by the work of Thomas and Znaniecki (1927) and developed into a legitimate research approach by the Chicago School of Sociology in the 1920s and 1930s, it was largely forgotten until recently resuscitated through the efforts of Goodson (1980, 1988, 1992), Sikes, Measor, and Woods (1985), and Woods (1984, 1985).

Although the term *method* denotes a singular approach to accessing data, life-history can involve a spectrum of strategies. Any document or artifact that may in some way describe a person's vision of the world is appropriate for analysis. For our purposes, we found lengthy, informal interviews most useful.

Life-histories from three teachers were gathered by means of multiple, lengthy interviews. The teachers received no compensation of any kind, but were required to travel a considerable distance for these repeated and time-consuming interviews. Our selection process was, therefore, restricted to people willing to volunteer large sums of personal time and share the full details of their lives as teachers. Participant selection criteria were sensitive to differences resulting from gender, school location, and race. The participants, therefore, included one woman and two men with one teacher each from urban, suburban, and rural schools. The latter criterion was not met as all the participating teachers were Caucasian.

Prior to the interviews, the three researchers selected themes and topics for framing, guiding, and focusing the interviews. It must be emphasized, however, that the interviews were open-ended and conversational to allow the interview to follow a path chosen by the teacher. We were after their stories in their words. Early sessions focused on experiences that brought them into teaching as well as their experiences as teachers. Later sessions were used to clarify or expand upon points made earlier and to check the accuracy of the researchers' interpretations. Each interview was conducted in private with only one teacher and one researcher present.

In keeping with an interpretive perspective and a focus on a specific career stage, extended, detailed histories were collected from three beginning teachers. The stories told by these teachers were compared and merged to identify themes and perspectives common in all three narratives. Comparing and contrasting the narratives of several teachers from differing settings seemed a logical strategy for reconstructing a clear, accurate, and reasonably trustworthy account of the teachers' perspective on induction. It must be recognized, however, that the three teachers were all unique individuals, as were their institutions. We searched for and reported only the common experiences among them, but the reader should be aware that differences also existed.

Themes were reconstructed from the interview text that provided insight into and understanding of the political realities of teacher induction from the teacher's viewpoint. We attempted to provide trustworthy interpretations by triangulating the three stories. This report contains only themes that were common to all three stories. Minimally, this meant that a theme was included when at least two teachers provided direct, quotable support for the theme. No theme was included if it appeared to contradict (directly or indirectly) any statements made by the third teacher. What emerged, we believe, were the common perspectives on a shared experience: the micropolitics of teacher induction as told by those who lived it.

The Teachers

Before we present the analysis and interpretations, the reader may find it helpful to know something of the three teachers herein described. These teachers all had less than 5 years of teaching experience. Pat had been teaching for 3 years, Marry was in his second year, and Chris was in her first year.

Interestingly, all three began their careers as part-time employees. After their first year as half-timers, Pat and Marry were hired full-time. Chris, being in her first year, was half-time when the study began, but midway through the year (and this study) she was informed that she would be offered a full-time position for the following year. Whether this theme is common among beginning teachers in the 1990s cannot be said with any certainty, but we found it to be a remarkable coincidence.

The authors suspected economic forces to be at work, for all three teachers believed themselves lucky to be employed. They reported difficulty in gaining their posts and cited examples of fellow teachers who had been unsuccessful in obtaining positions. Finally, our teachers were the only inductees (i.e., untenured teachers with less than 5 years of employment) in their schools. The tight job market, we believe, influenced the induction experienced by these teachers. The threat of job loss represented an important incentive to adopt conservative postures upon entering schools. Had teaching positions been abundant, the experience of induction would quite likely have been different for these teachers.

We recognized the possibility of economic conditions influencing teacher induction early in our study. When Marty came for his first interview, he had a pierced ear, but no earring. Before the interview began, he was asked out of concern "Did you loose your earring? .... No," he replied, "I just decided that a job was more important than an earring. So I took it out before my first interview and haven't had it in since." This pattern subtly repeated itself over the course of interviews with all three teachers.

None of our teachers reported any serious problems in coping with the requirements for teaching. All three seemed to experience what Huberman (1989) described as "easy beginnings." That is, they reported mostly positive relations with peers and students, manageable classes, a sense of pedagogical competence, and enthusiasm for their lives as teachers.

Although the three teachers graduated from the same university and all had majored in physical education, they did not know one another and their teaching responsibilities were in different subject areas. They taught in different school districts in the same state, but the districts were not in proximity. Below are their abbreviated biographies.

Pat Smith

Pat taught in Armut, the same city where he was born, raised, and attended college. Armut is a small, residential city on the West Coast with approximately 150,000 inhabitants. At Tomasa Junior High School, he taught health and physical education (PE) courses. In previous years he taught maths and science. He thought his position unique, for he saw students in a variety of educational contexts (classrooms, labs, and gymnasiums).

Pat had a keen interest in sport participation, particularly baseball, tennis, and basketball. He identified the long summer vacations awarded teachers as a prime job incentive, for it allowed him time to pursue his sport activities. His interest in sports led him into physical education and coaching. He considers being physically fit as one of his greatest assets as a teacher of health and PE. "I emulate the field. I look the part. I'm probably in the best shape of anybody on the staff. I give that healthy look every day I'm in school."

Pat had coached various sports in several area high schools and middle schools. Enjoying the contact with students, he credited his coaching with helping to develop effective class management techniques. He had also hoped that by coaching he could gain entry into a teaching position. In fact, because Pat coached her son, the person who assigned the district substitute teachers helped Pat gain employment.

One year after these interviews, Pat left teaching to sell insurance. He did not want to leave, but the lack of support for his efforts and having his contract terminated every year because of budget shortfalls gave him a sense of insecurity that eventually drove him from teaching. He explained: I'm getting older now,' and want to start a family. With the constant threat of losing my job because of budget cuts, I can't stay in teaching and plan for a future. It's too bad, because I really like teaching, especially the kids, but I have to put my family first.

Martin Bannister

Marry taught junior high school in Twin Lakes, an affluent suburb of a large, metropolitan city. At the time of this study, he was teaching three physical education classes, two maths classes, one health class, and was helping to coach the track teams. In his first year, he played a substitute role and split his time between two schools teaching whatever subject was required that day. By his second year he was a full-time teacher. He described the community where he teaches as "well-to-do" and reported satisfaction with both his position and his students.

Marry was an All-American track star in high school and eventually went to college on an athletic scholarship. The positive role modelling provided by his teachers convinced Marry that teaching was a profession in which he would be happy. "The summer of 1980 I went to Europe with a group of teachers, and my sister was starting school to become a teacher. I thought 'This is great. I'm going to be a teacher.' I never considered another career."

Shortly after these interviews, Marry received a study leave to return to school for his master's degree. His motives were threefold. First, his master's would complete the requirements for a permanent teaching certificate. Second, the degree would prepare him for the administrative role he wished to assume one day. Third, he could pursue his lifelong dream of preparing for and competing in the Olympic Games.

Marty's induction convinced him that his career choice was an appropriate one. After he earns his master's degree, he would like to resume his contact with children both in the classroom and on the athletic field. "I really, really want a highschool track coaching job where I call the shots. I really want that responsibility."

Chris Engel

Chris was a high school PE teacher in the rural community of Holtz. The 14 teachers of Holtz Central High School instruct a student body of approximately 140. One of Chris's classes had only 3 students. She began her first year as a part-time teacher. By the end of the year, the administrators were, according to Chris, so impressed with her teaching performance that they offered her a full-time contract. The year following our interviews, Chris reported that she was enjoying her full-time position.

Like Pat and Marty, it was Chris's love of the subject matter that carried her into teaching. Unlike Pat and Marty, physical education was the only subject Chris taught. Chris also coached softball for a high school in another school district. Chris's main avocation in life is softball. She played competitively in college and continues playing today. In addition to coaching a high school team, she also coaches an elite team of teenage girls in the summer. The latter team has qualified for national competition for the past 2 years.

Chris made her career decision at a young age. "My Mom says that I talked about becoming a physical education teacher ever since elementary school." Her sport experiences and PE classes influenced her decisions about the type of teacher she would become.

> I remember my role models were lazy, out-of-shape women. I always thought that when I'm a teacher I'm not going to ride my bike around the path while the students jog. I always wanted to be more involved.

Streams of Consciousness

Pat, Marty, and Chris revealed several factors that influenced and sustained their professional perspectives and practices. These factors varied in importance depending on the circumstance and situation. No one factor was overarching, nor was it possible to predict which factor would weigh most heavily in the teachers' thoughts or actions in any given moment. Most often it seemed that these factors were never very far from any of the teachers' decisions. Three interrelated themes emerged from the interview text: biography, role demands, and school culture.

The metaphor *streams of consciousness* was chosen because each of the three themes had multiple sources or tributaries that all flowed together to form the undercurrent directing the teachers' thoughts and actions (see Figure 1). The streams together poured into a reservoir of information teachers tapped when constructing a perspective or performing a teaching act.

These streams and tributaries do not represent an exhaustive list of all the influences shaping and sustaining these teachers. Rather, they encapsulate the influences and perspectives depicted in and shared among the stories told by the three teachers. We are reasonably confident that these streams represent the primary elements in the chemistry of school life for these teachers and, therefore, served as our blueprint for reconstructing the micropolitics of teacher induction.

Biography

Our beginning teachers carried three sets of baggage to their new place of employment. These included: (a) experiences that exercised similar or related pedagogical skills, (b) university coursework, and (c) experiences as a school pupil. The baggage became unpacked and used or stored and ignored depending on the interests of the teacher and the institution.

When describing resources for skills and knowledge used in teaching, the teachers most easily recalled related experiences. Chris, for example, found her student teaching experience the most beneficial aspect of her university education. She thought it valuable because it represented "actual time with the students. That's the biggest variable in teaching: the students and how you react to them." Similarly, Pat developed and selected classroom practices from extracurricular duties: "With my coaching background, I now have a pretty good management style with kids."

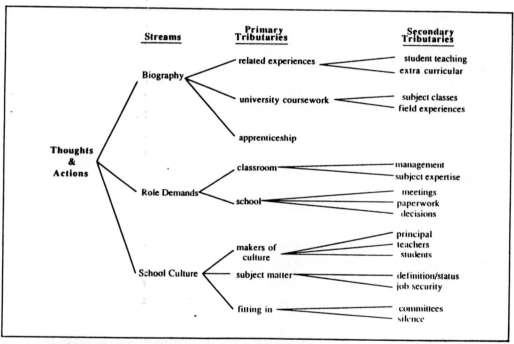

Figure 1. **Micropolitics of induction streams of consciousness**

Lottie (1975) theorized that students serve an apprenticeship-of-observation that later becomes an important information source for teachers practising the craft. In studying this theory, it was found that teachers began identifying, selecting, and evaluating pedagogical routines and practices while students in public schools (Schempp, 1989). Marty echoed this when reporting that his experiences as an athlete and student sculpted his teaching orientations and actions:

> *Outside the classroom they (teachers) were the coach or friend. Inside the classroom if I screwed up I was in trouble because of their expectations for me. They were very strict disciplinarians and they knew where to draw the line. That's really helped me as a teacher.*

Educational background, specifically university coursework, appeared to have its greatest value in supplying subject-matter content. Chris believed that "all my activity classes paid off. Those are invaluable." She claimed that most of the topics and activities she taught came directly from her subject classes. Pat too used subject-matter courses (or activity classes, as our teachers called them) as the foundation for his curricular decisions. Applicable and demonstrable teaching skills were also a by-product of Pat's coursework. In his words "taking activity classes; teaching techniques; learning to deal with kids, classroom strategies, classroom management; all those are very important."

The dependence upon activity or "practical" courses allowed the teachers to construct pedagogical routines and rituals fit for public schools. Translating philosophy into policy or extruding a teaching plan from a theory was more difficult and less economical. The press and grind of public school pedagogy required the beginning teachers to adopt professional perspectives that were practical (Clandinin & Connely, 1986; Elbaz, 1983) rather than intellectual (Giroux, 1988).

Perhaps the most useful aspects of education were sections of the preparation program that required contact with students in public schools. Marty taught three different subjects and drew from his teaching strategies classes often during his induction years. The strategies class required him to teach in public schools and then reflect on and judge those experiences. Learning to reflect helped him work through strategies he uses today. He also found the feedback he received from his peers, the professor, and his students useful in formulating a variety of teaching approaches.

Pat revealed a parallel perspective when he described his ideal teacher preparation program as revolving around subject-matter coursework and "getting out there in the school and working with kids." Coursework and experiences translating directly into classroom practices contained the most useful knowledge in the biographical warehouse of these teachers.

Interestingly, decisions regarding the occupational utility of a course seemed to be made while undertaking the course itself. Judgments regarding the worth of professional education courses were not reserved until one could attempt an application, nor were the opinions of the professor factored into decisions regarding the utility of course content. Previously formed perspectives encouraged aspiring teachers to discriminate between the useful and useless while still preparing to teach. Pat indicated: "1 had some philosophic differences with how the education department was run and how they were preparing me to teach. I was already working with kids, and I knew I could teach well."

The university education brought to schools by these new teachers held little currency with their seasoned peers. Marry put it this way:

> A lot of teachers who have taught for a long time think they have learned it all from experience and not from going to school. So if you are somebody new coming in, they think they need to train you to the ways of the real world.

The low status of a university preparation often led the beginning teachers to suppress and devalue their professional education. Marty continued:

> I think new teachers coming fresh out of school are so gung-ho. 1 know 1 was. You just want to get involved because you have all this knowledge that you just acquired that you want to tell somebody about. But, sometimes, that comes across as real arrogant to teachers who have been in the business for a long time.

There were times when education failed the beginning teachers, and they described these occasions as the difference between the university "ivory tower" and the "real world" of public schools. These events reinforced the low status of professional preparation and elevated experience as the real teacher of teachers. Pat related:

> *I think a good experience for me my first year was having to be creative. They didn't teach you that in the teacher preparation program. They never said that when you get our into the schools there may not be any equipment.*

Role Demands

The schools, communities, and subject areas served by our three teachers were all different. The occupational demands they faced, however, were alike. This was expected, for a profession such as teaching can often be defined by the services it provides as well as the tasks it undertakes (Schon, 1983). Similarities were also noted in the teachers' reactions and responses as they met the demands of their new roles.

Role demands were embodied in the expectations teachers faced in school (i.e., what they were supposed to do and how they were supposed to do it). Some of these demands were explicit (e.g., classroom management, grading) whereas others were more implicit (e.g., committee assignments, instructional style). The teachers had little choice but to meet the required demands, for failure to do so meant risking their jobs. Interestingly, these "explicit" demands were seldom made explicit, that is, it was simply assumed by all (administrators, peers, students, and the teachers themselves) that the new teacher would know what it was they were supposed to do and have a pretty good idea of how to do it. The demands were made explicit only when a difference in perception or assumption occurred (usually in varied forms of "We don't do that here" or "This is the way we have always done it"). The implicit demands were, for the most part, undertaken by choice, or at least appeared so. Failure to meet implicit demands adequately usually resulted in lowered status, which in turn could have led to the loss of one's position.

Zeichner et al. (1987) delineated the impact of school experience on teacher socialization into two levels: interactive (classroom) and institutional (school). Our teachers' narratives described these two contexts as holding unique and distinct tasks. Corresponding to Zeichner and his colleagues, our teachers located their occupational demands at both classroom and school levels.

Classroom

Descriptions of classroom demands faced by our teachers fit Doyle's (1986) portrayal of classroom tasks as revolving around two central structures: student learning and classroom management. And as Lortie (1975) noted, the duties of a teacher are the same on the first day of teaching as they are the last. Lacking routines worn comfortable by long practice and without the benefits of knowledge gained in years of experience, our teachers found the weight from their responsibilities heavy, and at times crushing. Marty began his teaching career like this:

> *The first day there was not much teaching going on. Our building has three levels. I have a basement class first period. Second period I have a class on the main floor. Third period I'm out in the gym. Fourth I'm back inside on the main floor. Fifth and sixth I'm in the gym again, and seventh period I'm back down in the*

basement. So this is my first day of taking attendance, learning the kids names, laying down basic rules and regulations, picking up everything I need, and getting to all my classes. Kids have all sorts of questions on the first day: "When do I eat lunch?", "When is this and when is that?" I'm still trying to figure out all those rules and regulations myself. My first class had 14 Spanish speaking kids and 2 English-speaking kids. I was trying to explain class rules to a bunch of kids that didn't understand English. This is my introduction, and I'm thinking "Oh God! I'm not going to make it!"

Our three teachers were in unanimous agreement that their first order of business and primary classroom responsibility was classroom management. Chris succinctly stated: "It's hard to teach anything until you have classroom management. A lot of my time was spent learning how to manage a classroom. Once you have that down, you can go from there." The micropolitics of induction quickly informed the teachers that their survival hinged upon gaining power over student actions. Student control was so essential to teaching that it served as a gate for screening teachers in and out of schools. Pat told this story:

I as half-time. Teaching PE, and there was a particular maths and science teacher who was really having trouble. I have a pretty good management style, so the principal asked if I would take over this teacher's class. Mainly what they needed was a classroom manager to get the class back under control. They had pretty much driven this guy to a nervous breakdown. I taught the last 6 weeks of that term and had the same assignment next term. It went great, and now I'm full-time.

More than simply managing children, the primacy of classroom management reflects the micropolitical reality of school life. Teachers are expected to establish themselves as authority figures over students (Waller, 1932). It is incumbent upon teachers to demonstrate the power and authority they hold over students to those outside the classroom (Feinman-Nemser & Floden, 1986). Establishing authority over students was essential for the new teacher to be accepted by all members of the school community. In response to the question "What have you had to do to be accepted as a teacher in this school?", Marty instinctively replied "Be firm and structured in my discipline." Success or failure, bluntly put, resided in the teacher's control over students: the greater the level of control, the greater the level of success.

Gaining power over students, although an important role demand, provided little personal satisfaction for the teachers in this study. Paradoxically, our teachers, like those in Lortie's (1975) study, found forging meaningful relationships with students to be their greatest reward. Although others defined teachers in terms of class control, our three teachers plumbed the essence of their role from another source. Pat explained: "I'm really a counsellor, a social worker, a friend, and a parent. It is a rewarding situation, but it is also a lot of work." Marty felt the same:"I want to be a sharing, giving person; a counsellor type. I've been able to do that."

If teachers derive their greatest satisfaction from caring for students and not dominating them, gaining power over students would classify as part of the regime of truth (Foucault, 1970) in schools. Put another way, teachers' control over students is a taken-for-granted assumption in schools. As can be seen in Pat's story, administrators, parents, peers, and even students see the teacher as the central authority figure in the classroom. Student control rests as the cornerstone of professional competence. This "truth" influenced the perspectives and actions of our three teachers and made it necessary for them to acquire tactics and negotiate for student control.

The primacy of management and the importance of interpersonal relationships had the side effect of marginalizing subject matter. Pat's move from part-time physical education teacher to full-time classroom teacher illustrates this point. That Pat was not a subject-matter specialist in the maths and science classes he assumed was subordinated to his skill in managing a classroom.

The classroom responsibilities facing the inductees had less to do with teaching children and more to do with juggling the multiple demands of a functioning institution. Reflecting on and articulating a given body of knowledge were secondary obligations for these beginning teachers. Other priorities took precedent. Marry explains:

> *I have to stay on top of all the paperwork I get in order to read it, fill it out properly, and give it to whoever I'm supposed to give it to. It seems like it really takes away from my organizational time to get lesson plans worked out to where I'd like them to be.*

Knowledge of the subject matter and ability to demonstrate this knowledge did serve as an avenue for gaining status in the school, particularly among students. Subject expertise (when available) was, however, more often used for establishing authority in the classroom than it was for furthering the education of students. As Pat reported, "You get a lot of respect from your kids when you are better than they are [in the subject area]. The teacher should be the expert."

Subject-matter expertise, although important, was still a distant second to the concern for student control. For example, two of the three teachers in this study were teaching in areas where they lacked experience, expertise, or certification; but all were considered good class managers.

School

Although the central tasks of our teachers were in classrooms, skilfully undertaking duties of school-wide consequence was also considered important. These duties were more of the implicit nature. That is, they were not formally required, but as we discovered, a teacher's participation or lack of participation held serious consequences for career development.

Meetings were a primary platform for executing school duties. Our teachers described numerous meetings with varying purposes (e.g., curricular, informational) and with various individuals (e.g., faculty, parents, administrators). Meetings served as important locations in the micropolitics of teacher induction. Because their work in classrooms isolated the teachers (Templin, 1988), meetings and school functions offered an opportunity to be viewed by colleagues, administrators, and others as part of the school culture. These events gave our teachers a visibility they could not achieve in their normal, daily course of duties. Marry believed his activities outside the classroom were essential to his acceptance into the school culture and explained that:

> *The social-political dynamics within a building are important in how you are viewed. The things that you do, that you get involved with, the staff functions, the committees you get on to do different things, really come into play in how you are viewed in the school.*

Comparatively, Chris found the watershed separating leaders from nonleaders among teachers was a "willingness to get involved."

Extraneous duties conspired, at times, to make the newcomer's life difficult. It was not one single duty that stood alone as troublesome, but the multitude thrust on them. To the question "What makes teaching hard?", Marty answered:

The paperwork The administration. Oh God, they just nickel and dime you with this form and that procedure. It's unbelievable. Every time you turn around there is a new form to fill out on this kid who has a counselling appointment, or this kid who is allergic to bees, or pulling together homework for this kid who is absent from school, or this kid who is going to a special class, or this kid who just got suspended. Every day you have five or six pieces of paper. And now, we don't like the way this works so we're going to change this form or how we do that. Just about the time you figure it out, along comes somebody to change it.

The number of decisions, the variety of tasks, and the immediacy of the demands forced the novice teachers to use instinctive reactions, adopt time-honoured traditions and management routines, and import lessons from related experiences. The fluid, immediate, and dynamic pressures of school life did not permit teachers time to reflect deeply on a problem before attempting a solution. The reflexive responses required to maintain class momentum, satisfy the needs of a diverse student body, and adapt to scheduling and procedural changes left no time for our teachers to recall university lectures, consult their colleagues, or review pertinent professional literature. The role demands embodied in the micropolitics of induction created a situation where, as others have noted (Burlingame, 1972; Lortie, 1975), the teachers felt they succeeded or failed alone, as Marty related:

It seemed like for the first 3 or 4 weeks it never ended. At the end of the day I felt like I had been on my feet for 20 days straight. I felt like I had to make a decision every 5 seconds. Probably more than half of them were wrong. It was tough.

School Culture

It is in the micropolitics of teacher induction that newcomers learn the traditions and trademarks, the codes of culture, that give meaning and purpose to the established practices and patterns of daily school life. The school culture comprises the rules that define what is normal, acceptable, and legitimate in terms of acting and thinking in the school. In discussing the culture of her school, Chris remarked:

I'm still trying to figure it out, but they're [the people in the school] kind of old-fashioned. But, I like the small school setting for teaching. No one skips class because they would get caught. So kids don't skip class and they're not late for class.

Within the codes of culture resides the notion of power. The micropolitics of induction instructed our three teachers in both the distribution and appropriation of power within their school. In the process, these teachers learned who held power (e.g., administrators, "involved" teachers) and the ways and means of appropriating the necessary power to secure their position in the school culture. Marty described the power distribution in the culture of one school this way:

I was in two buildings last year. This building that I'm in now accepted me as an educator from day one. The other building didn't. It was like you're not a regular teacher until you've been in the business for 10 years. It was the aura of the building.

Definitions of school culture and teaching culture are many and varied. Sparkes (1989) emphasized the contested, dynamic nature of school culture:

The patterns of understandings, which newcomers must grasp, make up the various cultures of teaching and form a process of reality construction that enable individuals to see and understand particular events, objects, language, and situations in distinctive ways. Hence, teacher cultures are embodied in the work-related beliefs and knowledge that they share, which includes beliefs about the appropriate ways of acting on the job, what is rewarding in teaching, and the "craft knowledge" that enables teachers to do their work. Importantly, these patterns of understandings also provide a basis for making the individuals' behaviour meaningful, and culture should be viewed as an active living phenomenon through which teachers create and recreate the worlds in which they live. (p. 319-320)

Although biography served as a starting point in defining our teachers' practices and perspectives, school culture took on an increasingly important role as the inductees attempted to gain veteran status. Cultural codes became particularly pronounced in situations where job security was an important consideration (and for our teachers, this was *very* important).

In our analysis, two things became evident. First, the cultural codes, or regimes of truth (to borrow from Foucault, 1970), were informally passed to the newcomer by other members of the culture, usually during informal school meetings. The bearers of these cultural messages included administrators, colleagues, and students. The causal, interactional nature of these *culture lessons* told the novice, as Chris put it, "how things really worked in the school."

Second, embedded within these codes were ways of thinking and acting that were intended to serve the inductee as they ascended the member status hierarchy. The micropolitics of teacher induction required that the newcomer learn the roles played by each actor in the culture, comprehend the messages these people bore, and adopt and devise strategies for gaining the influence necessary to insure his or her survival in the school.

In explaining the role of school culture in the micropolitics of induction, the narratives of our three teachers seemed to focus on three areas: the makers of school culture, the definition of subject matter shaped in the school culture, and finally the strategies used to affiliate with the established culture. These shall be addressed in turn.

Makers of School Culture

The makers of school culture included administrators, teachers (including the inductees), and students. Among them, they constructed the norms that constituted the cultural codes of the school. Although schools were not immune to influence from parents, communities, and the larger society, our teachers focused almost exclusively on primary members when describing the school's culture. Our analysis was, therefore, confined to these groups: administrators, colleagues, and students.

Behavioural and attitudinal norms were not formally and directly conveyed to beginning teachers, perhaps because these norms contained a degree of flexibility and were not clearly articulated. Foucault (1980) noted that regimes of truth are rarely formalized but simply taken for granted. That is the source of their influence and ideological control. The codes of school culture (i.e., the accepted ways of acting, seeing, and believing) were often passed to the novice in the form of "stories." Chris told us:

I hear stories from students and teachers about teachers who were released the year before. The art teacher, last year, shaved his head and let the kids paint on it. It was something a little too radical for a small town like this, and so he was out the next year.

The hierarchy of power in the school was clear to all three of our teachers. Principals and administrators held the greatest power, followed by teachers, and then students. The beginning teachers' status was fixed within the teacher group, but our three teachers negotiated the terms and conditions of their status with all three groups.

Administrators. The individuals holding the greatest power over the inductees were administrators. Chris reported an incident early in her career in which the teachers and principal were in direct disagreement over the issue of class scheduling. The principal prevailed, and Chris remembers that the incident "pointed out who really has the control: Administrators do."

In every case we studied, the principal was instrumental in obtaining full-time employment for the teachers. In return, these teachers were grateful and loyal. Pat confessed that:

I'm a little worried about [budget cuts] next year. But I have some level of confidence because the principal and vice-principal are behind me and want me in that school. I got laid off last year, but the principal told me that she really wanted me back and she was going to do everything she could to get me back, and she did.

Administrators use the codes of the school culture to select and retain new teachers. Our teachers were well aware of these codes and attempted to remain within these expectations for behaviour, appearance, and attitude. Often times these codes had less to do with educating students and more to do with what Ginsberg (1987) called the *ideology of professionalism:* looking professional. Chris noted: "I really think what eventually got me a job was how I looked. My physical appearance and dress appealed to the superintendent. He's real big on appearance."

Administrative influence reached into conceptions and definitions of subject matter as well. Marty said:

He [the principal] is not real big on what you are teaching, in any subject. He doesn't care what it is, but rather how you deal with kids. He believes that every kid that comes into our building should have a chance to go through a program that is nurturing, where the kid feels comfortable and positive. So I guess that's subject matter.

The administrators also served as brokers between influences and regulations from outside the school and the beginning teacher. For example, a mandate or information from the school board, state educational agencies, and sometimes even parents was screened by administrators and then passed along to the teacher, usually with a comment regarding its relative importance.

Colleagues. Peer teachers form another influential group for the beginning teacher. Established teachers hold a vested interest in the induction of new teachers, for the newcomer may soon be one among them: friend or foe. These teachers played active roles in the micropolitics of induction by helping newcomers make the transition into the culture of the school in ways that preserved their own sets of interests (Ball, 1987).

The teachers of this study described incidents in which their colleagues identified important tasks, guided curricular decisions, and informed the beginner of his or her status in the school. In describing her initial contact with a colleague, Chris reported that he" was kind of showing me around. We looked over the course outlines and how he graded." Later discussions included disciplinary policies, curriculum schemes, administrative practices, and teaching styles.

Veteran teachers have established traditions and perceptions that the novice must accept, reject, modify, or accommodate. Sometimes the newcomer walked a thin line between alienating these teachers and injecting his or her own brand of pedagogy. It surprised us to discover the consistency among our teachers in finding "uncaring colleagues"; teachers burned-out or simply too busy for matters pertaining to the education of children. In the face of apathy, our teachers simply went their own way with little fear of reprisal. Marty said: "One of the other teachers could care less. He's retiring and has been retired for 20 years, everyone says. The principal told me that when Harry retires, I can shore up the program and make it viable." Chris had a similar story:

> We looked over everything: courses, grading procedures, and everything else. I didn't agree with some of it. We compromised and changed some things. He thought it would be a good idea if we were consistent. He didn't really care what we did. Of course, I got to retype all the changes.

Although our teachers found it important to appease their peers and demonstrate a willingness to conform to institutional norms and standards, colleagues did not seem a particularly powerful socializing agent in terms of pedagogical practice or beliefs. Chris perceived that, professionally, she and her partner "are more independent. It is a supportive relationship." The characterization of collegial relationships as "supportive but independent" was consistent with other teacher socialization research (Burlingame, 1972; Zeichner et al., 1987).

Colleagues can, however, ease (or perhaps prevent, which did not occur among our teachers) a novice's entry into the school culture. Chris said:

> He doesn't help me as a teacher, but he helps me deal with the administration. For example, if he hears the towels have been left out, he'll tell me because he likes me. If he didn't like me, he wouldn't tell me, and I'd get in trouble.

Students. Students played a discernible role in formulating and communicating the codes of school culture. Winning over student respect and gaining acceptance as a teacher were essential requirements for successful teacher induction. Pat said:

> You can tell that they [students] respect you; they look up to you; they look forward to seeing you. I've had some comments from parents about how they really appreciate the job I'm doing with their kids. Kids thank me for what I'm doing, and that's the feedback you get that you like to hear.

When student expectations meshed with peer and administrator expectations, the standards of the school culture, however implicit, became clear to the beginning teacher. Marty learned an important pedagogical lesson from students in an early class that taught him to capture discipline with instruction:

> A lot of kids were taking advantage of me, thinking "He's close to our age, so we can screw around." So I jumped up on a chair and started giving my lecture— dead silence. I'll never forget the difference. So that has always stuck in my head

that it's really important for a teacher to be creative and do different things with students that gets their attention and makes them listen.

Besides reinforcing the primacy of classroom management, students also conveyed their perceptions of subject-matter importance. In almost all cases, our teachers did not find students wanting an education. To the contrary, our teachers reported students uninterested in learning. Chris said: "They [students] are always looking for the easy way out. They are not really willing to study at home. If it sounds like fun, they might do it." Pat had a similar perception, but felt it was sometimes justified because

Kids just have so much more to deal with today. How can you expect students to come in and learn algebra when they are going home and Mom and Dad are selling cocaine, or Mom and Dad are alcoholics, or Mom is in prison? We've got about one third of our kids on the school lunch program, which means they can't afford to buy their own lunch.

All three of our teachers believed that the general lack of interest and motivation for learning they saw in their students was directly traceable to the childrens' home environment.

Students provided important benchmarks for novices to gauge their success. The teachers received immediate and continuous feedback regarding their pedagogical abilities from students. In the isolated confines of a classroom, this feedback strongly influenced the young teacher's sense of competence and professional value. Marty pridefully relayed this story:

I have an eighth grader in two of my classes. He's such a street kid. They think he is involved in gangs and selling drugs. It's not my place to judge. I've been working with him independently. He stays with me after school to do homework and to help me. And for the first time, he passed all his classes. He only has four classes, but he passed them all, for the first time.

Importance of Subject Matter

School culture also provided norms by which subject matter was accorded status and prestige. The teachers in our study were convinced that their actions and beliefs influenced the status granted their subject area. That is, the way teachers perceived their subject and conveyed those perceptions influenced the perceptions others held of their subject. Chris recalled

filling in for the other PE teacher one afternoon and several girls asked to leave to work on a poster. I asked if it was an emergency project that was due. They said no. They perceived PE as unimportant and that if you had something else you wanted to do, you could do it during PE. I think it reflected the other teacher's attitude.

The induction of our newcomers taught them that in the scheme of school culture, subject matter was not among the higher priorities. Classroom management, school politics, and meeting the childrens' social and emotional needs all usurped the importance of subject knowledge. Our teachers fit the profile Lacey (1989, p. xv) described as "emphasizing the welfare of the child above the interest of their subject." Pat explained:

There was one student who had some abuse going on at home, and the only place this person had to go was a 24-hour supermarket. It was midnight, and this was a lighted place, it was warm, she felt safe there, and it was open. A 24-hour supermarket! And she had to go to school the next day. People don't realize that you're not just there teaching subject matter: You're a consultant, a confidant, a social worker. You might be the only bright face and positive person that the kid sees all day. So a lot of times the subject matter takes a back seat to just getting the kid in class, giving them a positive experience, and making them feel good about themselves.

Physical education has historically shared the lowest rung on the subject matter status ladder with the likes of art, music, and home economics (Evans & Williams, 1989). Being trained as physical education specialists proved particularly problematic for our teachers. Hired to teach multiple subjects, initial part-time employment, and the threat of reduced class offerings in times of financial crises all conspired to relegate the subject of physical education—and by virtue of association, our teachers—to the bottom of the academic hierarchy. When budgets became tight and reductions needed to be made, or when curriculum innovations were initiated, the perception of physical education as having low status and being unimportant to the mission of the school magnified the teachers' already low status as inductees and put our teachers particularly at risk of losing their positions. Pat told us:"During the summer the leadership team got together, which is made up of administrators and a few teachers. They decided to drop three PE classes. So we're down three PE classes from what we had last year."

Students subtly conveyed the message that they did not necessarily consider physical education an important subject either. According to Chris, the students simply wanted a good time when they came to PE. Marry noted the same reactions and tried to reverse this belief, but reported mixed success:

I have an eighth-grade class that says every Friday "Hey, how come we're not playing a game?" I tell them that we are in a particular unit and this is what we are supposed to be learning. I'm still pulling teeth with them. Well, there's a new sheriff in town. My seventh graders love it.

The economic climate can couple with low status to force beginning teachers to forsake the defence of their subject area in favour of a more important consideration: job security. Pat told us:

My colleagues wrote a letter to the administration about the importance of PE and asking why we were dropping classes and cutting the PE budget. I told them I couldn't sign it because of my (untenured)] position. It's a real touchy situation and I'm right in the middle. 1 don't want to alienate my colleagues, but I want to have a job.

The three teachers all reported that they felt accepted in the school culture, were reasonably secure in their positions (exclusive of budget cuts), and believed they were held in relatively high esteem by colleagues (exclusive of subject matter). Yet, the investigators wondered how much of this perception was influenced by the fact that in the previous year two of the teachers had been only part-time employees, and Chris felt lucky to have a job at all. There exists the strong possibility that the teachers felt positive about their positions because (a) they very much liked what they were doing, (b) the line between employment and unemployment was very fragile, and (c) they all felt fortunate to be employed as teachers.

Fitting in

Colleagues, students, and administrators can exert enormous pressure on beginning teachers (Zeichner et al., 1987). These groups, collectively and individually, inform teachers about the cultural codes, regimes of truth, or standards of the profession that drive the form and function of the school. In these, newcomers learn the expectations for their actions, attitudes, and demeanour.

These lessons in culture are about how a teacher presents him or herself, as an individual, in the school. Thus, understanding and adapting to school culture can be quite distinct from (although certainly related to) learning to teach children in classrooms. Every established group or institution holds certain cultural norms, for it is within these norms that a group achieves identity and distinction. Newcomers must subscribe to the prevailing ways of the group.

Our teachers believed professional survival was contingent on their ability to prove that they understood and embraced the cultural norms of the school. This is not to say that they agreed with every policy or philosophy encountered or attempted to follow every directive or suggestion given. Rather, they believed it necessary to demonstrate their uniqueness as individuals, while at the same time to avoid violating the cultural norms of the school. In short, our teachers felt compelled to prove they fit with the group.

The teachers recounted several strategies for fitting in. A common strategy among them was joining committees. Curriculum committees were preferable, for they allowed novices to learn routines and requirements for classroom life while simultaneously providing a stage for demonstrating their eagerness to fit. Lacey (1977) termed this *strategic compliance.* Marry described the strategy thusly:

> *I just get involved in whatever I can. I go and sit and listen and learn and don't contribute anything unless somebody asks me "Well, what do you think?" It shows that I am willing to just come in and be a part of something rather than wanting to come in and take over.*

By far the most prevalent and dominant strategy used to fit in was to remain silent. The three teachers were unanimous in their regard for this strategy. To show their willingness to fit in and accept the status quo, the beginning teachers formed a society of the silent. That is, they were afraid to express opinions to peers and administrators that might be considered controversial and thus jeopardize their chances for success and survival in the school. Pat observed that "Teachers are not very subject to change; they are used to having what they had in the past. They don't change very much." Chris put it this way: "I've been real quiet. I don't want to cause a lot of friction. I'm trying to feel out the situation, and I don't want to cause any bad vibes. I want to have a job." Marty put it more bluntly: "I just try to keep my mouth shut."

Discussion

The purpose of this study was to reconstruct the micropolitics of teacher induction from the experiences of three beginning teachers. In reading this account, it is our hope that others navigating the tricky waters of teacher induction may draw insights to aid them in their quest to educate. We hope too that this study induces others to consider, reflect on, and perhaps question critically the professional induction of teachers.

In the course of this study, we found subject matter to be problematic; very few seemed concerned for its health and welfare in schools. Marty found students appreciated good teaching, but confessed that other role responsibilities diverted his attention. Pat won his mathematics position not because of his subject expertise (of which he had little), but because of his skill as a classroom manager. Teachers' status was measured in student control and matters removed from classroom instruction.

The teachers in this study reported that because of inexperience, they needed more time to prepare good lessons. They were also puzzled over the lack of interest and respect given to their subject matter by members of the school community. Administrators and colleagues who were concerned and competent in a subject matter and its pedagogy were greatly appreciated but few in number. The students' role in teacher induction proved significant, and we believe the micropolitics of induction would have been radically different if the students our teachers faced walked into classrooms demanding an education rather than counselling or entertainment. Schools are not likely to provide the educational services critics are demanding until subject matter is accorded a higher priority than it currently receives in public schools.

The current micropolitical climate faced by inductees devalued and discounted the professional preparation received at universities. Attempts to reform schools by reforming university-based teacher education programs seem, therefore, to have only a limited prospect for success. Teachers entering school cultures that require compliance and silence find little incentive to offer suggestions for improving those schools and risk placing themselves in great peril by alienating colleagues with reform proposals brought from university teacher education programs. From the findings of this study, we are inclined to agree with those who advocate a sharing of responsibility for teacher education and collaborative efforts that call for meaningful and enduring connections between the presently separated worlds of universities and public schools (e.g., Holmes Group, 1986).

The three teachers we studied were so pleased to have a teaching position that they were not inclined to complain about the conditions of employment or their induction. When Pat was asked to describe his major success in teaching to date, he replied without hesitation: "Getting a job." We are, therefore, particularly pessimistic in these burdensome economic times about improving schools with a fresh tide of teachers. When employment is difficult to obtain, having a job, regardless of the conditions, is generally preferable to having no job at all. Economic conditions appear likely to continue to pressure new teachers to forsake their ideals and education and accept the conditions and standards of the schools as they presently exist. Until probationary periods encourage teachers to think reflectively and critically and to experiment with reform proposals, we cannot look to a new corps of teachers entering schools each year to improve educational standards. In the current micropolitical climate of schools, teachers and students alike are short-changed. New initiatives and the professional development of novice and veteran teachers alike are curbed, and, consequently, students seldom benefit from teachers eager and enthusiastic with new solutions to old educational problems.

If schools are to change, teacher induction will need to change. One change that we see as essential is allowing beginning teachers to express themselves more freely without fear of condemnation, reprisals, or job loss. This should not be taken to mean that the knowledge and beliefs veteran teachers have won through years of service and experience should be summarily dismissed, but rather, this study leads us to believe that new teachers must be encouraged not simply to fit in but to experiment and develop pedagogical practices and responsive perspectives that place student learning and welfare at the forefront of concerns. They also must be encouraged to reflect critically on what it means to teach in public schools, to interrogate, challenge, and change the structures of schooling that constrain the essential missions of schools (Sparkes, 1991). Teachers should realize that they can change the conditions in which they operate, and this realization must commence with induction.

If the aspirations, inspirations, and education new teachers carry to their work place are to benefit students and schools, teachers will need institutional support to move ideas into action, test alternatives, question current conditions, and refine their craft. Perhaps in an air of acceptance and encouragement, new teachers can show less concern for fitting in to current school cultures and more concern for the children and society schools were built to serve.

Note

The authors are grateful to Harry F. Wolcott for his helpful suggestions regarding data analysis.

References

Ball, S. (1987). *The micropolitics of the school.* London: Methuen.

Burlingame, M. (1972). Socialization constructs and the teaching of teachers. *Quest, 18* (spring), 40-56.

Clandinin, D., & Connelly, F. (1986). Rhythms in teaching: The narrative study of personal practical knowledge of classrooms. *Teaching and Teacher Education, 2*(4), 377-387.

Doyle, W. (1986). Classroom organization and management. In M.C. Wittrock (Ed.), *Handbook of research on teaching* (3rd ed., pp. 392-431). New York: Macmillan. Elbaz, F. (1983). *Teacher thinking: A study of practical knowledge.* London: Croom Helms.

Evans, J., & Williams, T. (1989). Moving up and getting out: The classed and gendered career opportunities of physical education teachers. In T. Templin & P. Schempp (Eds.), *Socialization into physical education: Learning to teach* (pp. 235-249). In-dianapolis: Benchmark. Ewert, G.D. (1991). Habermas and education: A comprehensive overview of the influence of Habermas in educational literature. *Review of Educational Research, 61,*345-378.

Feinman-Nemser, S., & Floden, R. (1986). The cultures of teaching. In M.C. Wittrock (Ed.), *Handbook of research on teaching* (3rd ed., pp. 505- 526). New York:

Macmillan. Foucault, M. (1970). *The order of things: An archaeology of the human sciences.* New York: Vintage Press. Foucault, M. (1980). *Power/Knowledge.* New York: Pantheon.

Ginsburg, M. (1987). Reproduction, contradiction, and conceptions of professional: The case of pre-service teachers. In T. Popkcwitz (Ed.), *Critical studies in teacher education* (pp. 86-129). Lewes, England: Falmcr.

Giroux, H. (1988). *Teachers as intellectuals: A pedagogy for the opposition.* South Hadley, MA: Bergin & Garvey.

Goodson, I. (1980). Life histories and the study of schooling. *Interchange, 1* 1(4), 62-76.

Goodson. 1. (1988). *The making of curriculum.* Lewes, England: Falmer Press.

Goodson, 1. (Ed.). (1992). *Studying teachers' lives.* New York: Teachers College Press.

Habermas, J. (1981). *Theorie des kommunikativen Handelns (Band 1): Handlungsra- tionalitat und gesellschaftliche Rationalisierung.* Frankfurt am Main: Suhrkamp.

Holmes Group. (1986). *Tomorrow's teachers: A report of the Holmes group.* East Lansing, MI: Author.

Hoyle, E. (1982). Micropolitics and educational organizations. *Educational Management and Administration,* 10(1), 87-98.

Huberman, M. (1989). The professional life cycle of teachers. *Teachers College Record,* 91(1), 31-57.

Lacey, C. (1977), *The socialization of teachers.* London: Methuen.

Lacey, C. (1989). Foreword. In T. Templin & P. Schempp (Eds.), *Socialization into physical education: Learning to teach* (p. xv). Indianapolis: Benchmark Press.

Lortie, D.C. (1975). *Schoolteacher.* Chicago: University of Chicago Press.

Marsick, V. (1989, March). *Learning to be: Life history and professionalization.* Paper presented at the American Educational Research Association Annual Meeting, San Francisco, CA.

Schempp, P.G. (1989). The apprenticeship-of-observation in physical education. In T. Templin & P. Schempp (Eds.), *Socialization into physical education: Learning to teach* (pp. 13-38). Indianapolis: Benchmark Press.

Schempp, P.G., & Graber, K.C. (1992). Teacher socialization from a dialectical perspective: Pretraining through induction. *Journal of Teaching in Physical Education,* 11(4), 329-348.

Schon, D.A. (1983). *The reflective practitioner.. How professionals think in action.* New York: Basic Books.

Sikes, P., Measor, L., & Woods, P. (1985). *Teacher careers: Crises and continuities.* Lewes, England: Falmer Press.

Sparkes, A.C. (1989). Culture and ideology in physical education. In T. Templin & P. Schempp (Eds.), *Socialization into physical education: Learning to teach (pp. 315-338).* Indianapolis: Benchmark Press.

Sparkes, A.C. (1991). The culture of teaching, critical reflection, and change: Possibilities and problems. *Educational Management and Administration, 19(1), 4-19.*

Thomas, W., & Znaniecki, F. (1927). The *Polish peasants in Europe and America.* Chicago: University of Chicago Press.

Templin, T. (1988). Teacher isolation: A concern for the collegial development of physical educators. *Journal of Teaching in Physical Education, 7,* 197-207.

Veeneman, S. (1984). Perceived problems of beginning teachers. *Review of Educational Research,* 54(2), 143-178.

Wolcott, H. (1990). *Writing up qualitative research.* Newbury Park, CA: Sage.

Woods, P. (1984). Teacher, self and curriculum. In I. Goodson and S. Ball (Eds.), *Defining curriculum: Histories and ethnographies.* Lewes, England: Falmer Press.

Woods, P. (1985). Conversations with teachers. *British Educational Research Journal,* 11(1), 13-26.

Zeichner, K., & Gore, J. (1990). Teacher socialization. In R. Houston (Ed.), *Handbook of research on teacher education* (pp. 329-348). New York: Macmillan.

Zeichner, K., Tabachnick, B., & Densmore, K. (1987). Individual, institutional, and cultural influences on the development of teachers' craft knowledge. In J. Calderhead (Ed.), *Exploring teachers' thinking* (pp. 21-59). London: Cassell Educational Ltd.